An Illustrated History of
PLYMOUTH'S
RAILWAYS

By
Martin Smith

Laira Junction signalbox, undated. This box must surely have controlled more engine and train movements than any other in the Plymouth area. In this 'signalman's eye view', No.5003 LULWORTH CASTLE hauls an up stopper. PHOTOGRAPH: R.C. RILEY

IRWELL
PRESS ≋

First Published in the United Kingdom by
IRWELL PRESS 1995
P.O.Box 1260, Caernarfon, Gwynedd, LL55 3ZD
Printed in Huddersfield by The Amadeus Press

Contents

Acknowledgements

During the preparation of this book, a wealth of invaluable advice and assistance was provided by Messrs. Eric Youldon and Bill Peto. Sincere thanks to you both. An especial thanks to Ken Coventry, and thanks also to Paul Burkhalter, Alan Lathey, Chris Hawkins and George Reeve, and to my wife, Micky - despite being unable to tell a Bulleid Pacific from a lavatory brush, she has somehow managed to seem enthusiastic about this project.
Martin Smith,
Coleford, Somerset, April 1995.

Introduction

The history of Plymouth's railways, especially the corporate fisticuffs between the broad gauge companies and the LSWR camp, is very involved. It would be a little over-ambitious to attempt a wholly complete history of the subject in a modest little book such as this and instead, the text is, to a great extent, an unpretentious collection of material from various primary sources.

In an attempt to come up with something a little different, many hours have been spent delving through assorted official documents - railway company committee minutes, Board of Trade reports, accident investigations, and the rest. It is hoped that the end result will appeal even to the veterans of railway lore.

For the purpose of this book, the geographical boundaries are Laira and Plymstock to the east and the Royal Albert Bridge in the west - subjects such as the Yealmpton branch and Tavistock Junction are therefore excluded.

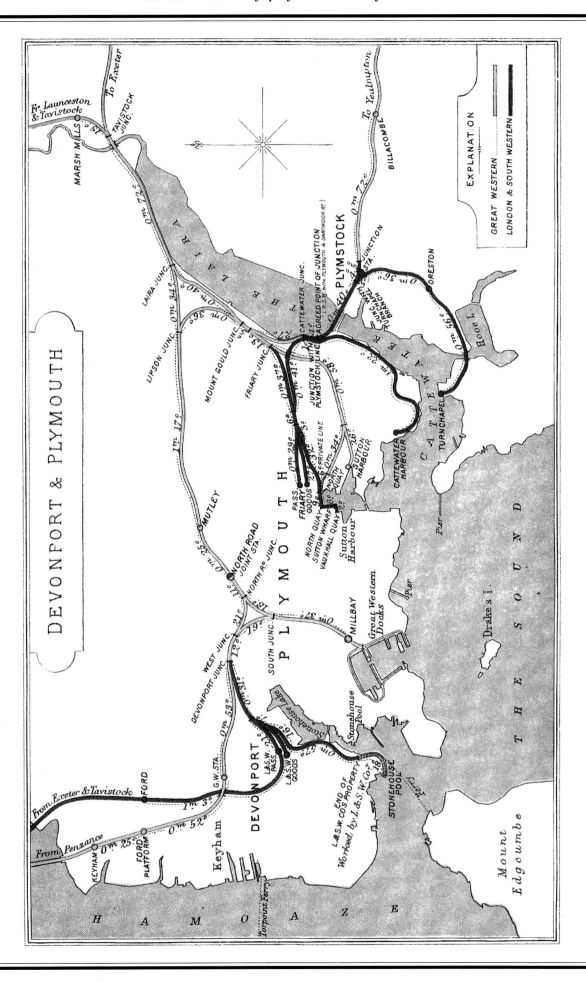

Sketch Map of
PLYMOUTH'S RAILWAYS

Chapter One
GWR and Before
'...in some respects an objectionable station...'

On 5 May 1848 the South Devon Railway opened its line from Exeter as far as a temporary station at Laira Green, but the railway was not extended into the centre of Plymouth until the following year. The SDR's original idea had been for a terminus at Eldad, but that was superseded by plans for a terminus on the south side of Union Street at Millbay. Even the Millbay scheme had to be amended - the SDR originally wanted to take the line across Union Street on the level, but that proposal did not curry favour with the Board of Trade.

The extension from Laira Green to Millbay was completed in March 1849, and was inspected by the Board of Trade on the 28th. The line was laid double throughout and was 'in every respect ready for the conveyance of the public', but the Inspector recommended that 'a signal be erected to be worked with a wire, so as to stop all trains coming from Plymouth in the event of any vehicles crossing the Dartmoor Railway'. (This last-named was a horse-worked line between Sutton Harbour and Princetown). The South Devon, the BoT Inspection papers recount, 'were about to erect a signal which would be seen some distance down the line, which with careful driving may

be sufficient', but in consideration of the steep incline falling towards the Dartmoor Railway, it was considered that a 'well-placed signal, worked by a wire' would, by being seen from four hundred yards further, 'add much to the security of the traffic on the Railway'.

The terminus lay at the end of a level space 14 chains in length, immediately at the foot of a mile-long incline, on a gradient varying from 1 in 124 to 1 in 63. This could be worked with safety, the Board of Trade concluded, but it would require 'great care and attention on the part of those entrusted with the management of the trains', for in the event of the 'breaks' (the contemporary spelling) being 'overpowered', the trains 'would be brought to a dead stand, having no rails beyond the station upon which they could proceed'. The Millbay extension opened to passenger traffic on Monday 2 April 1849, and to goods on 1 May.

In subsequent years, the BoT was somewhat unenthusiastic about the arrangements at Millbay. Following an accident there in December 1865, Colonel Yolland described the potentially hazardous methods of working: *'Plymouth station is in some respects an objectionable station, and limited for*

accommodation, although it has of late years been materially enlarged and improved; but the engines of all incoming passenger trains that arrive at the ticket platform [which opened in August 1851] *at the East side of the down line are there detached, run ahead, and are then shunted back out of the way, while a pilot engine comes out from the engine shed siding, situated on the western side of the railway and north of the ticket platform, crosses over the up main line and thence on to the down main line to the rear of the passenger train, which it then pushes forward from the ticket to the station platform, no very great distance, it is true, but involving the objectionable practice of pushing the train from behind, and also necessitating the bringing out of another engine from the engine shed siding, or causing the train engine to run round the train, which operations would be entirely unnecessary if provision had been made in laying out the station for the train engine, taking the train on to the station platforms without uncoupling.*

'The switchman who calls the pilot engine out from the engine shed siding is provided with up and down distant signals to protect the pilot engine while in the act of crossing from the

Generations of holidaymakers passed through Plymouth in their annual rush to the Cornish Riviera, and consequently missed the numerous attractions which Plymouth itself had to offer. One such attraction was the Tinside open air swimming pool beneath the Hoe - the pool was opened in 1933 to replace separate, smaller pools for men, women and children. The Hoe - out of view behind the promenade on the top left of the picture - is itself one of the city's great attractions; it was once referred to as 'the great lung of Plymouth'. The large building on the hill is the Marine Biological Institution, and behind it are the walls of the Citadel; out of view on the other side of the hill is Sutton Harbour.

Plymouth's most famous son is Sir Francis Drake, although he actually came from Tavistock. Drake's statue, unveiled in 1884 on the Esplanade at Plymouth, was in fact a replica of one at Tavistock. The Promenade, seen here behind the statue, was constructed in the late 1880s; during World War II open-air dances were held here - a great morale booster to the embattled citizens of Plymouth. One of the houses in the picture was the Plymouth home of Lord and Lady Astor - she was the first woman M.P., and he was the Lord Mayor of Plymouth during World War II.

engine shed siding to the down main line, and for preventing an out-going train from leaving the platforms until this up distant signal is set at "all right". I am, however, informed that, in practice, the drivers of passenger trains do not look to this up distant signal at all, but to an up signal attached to the switches of a through back road, situated at the south end of the ticket platform, which is worked by the yard signalman, whose post is near the ticket platform, in accordance with the indications of the up distant signal worked by the engine shed switchman'.

It will be noted in the above report that Millbay station was referred to as 'Plymouth'. The title of Millbay was not actually applied until 1 May 1877, soon after the opening of the new station at North Road, of which more anon.

The accident which prompted the above criticism had occurred on 16 December 1865: the 5.10pm up Launceston train had reached the ticket platform about 7.05am and immediately the train stopped the engine shed 'switchman' altered the 'switches', and signalled by hand lamp to the driver of the pilot to come out from the engine shed siding, and to proceed across to the down main, in the fashion described above, in order to push the Launceston train from the ticket station platform. The driver sounded the whistle, and started immediately, as he was accustomed to do, but before his engine reached the crossing, the switchman, to his horror no doubt, saw the 6.30pm down Cornwall passenger train approaching from the station platform on the main line. He then, in the dry

language of the Report, 'showed a red light towards the pilot engine' - the driver did all in his power to stop, but the loco fouled the up main line, and 'a collision immediately ensued'.

In front of the pilot, and attached to it, were three vehicles, a 'carriage truck' and two vans; this 'carriage truck', which was next to the engine, and the van next to it were thrown off

the rails and, together with the pilot engine were 'a good deal damaged'. Matters were made even worse by an evil fate: *'The other van, by the shock of the collision, became detached, and ran down the steep incline of 1 in 63, and came into collision with the last vehicle of the Launceston train then standing alongside the ticket platform, but not doing much damage to*

Millbay station, probably early 1900s. It is easy to suggest that the picture of the station's Millbay Road frontage is circa 1880-1890, but the electric tram wires are a give-away. Trams (horse-drawn) came to Plymouth in the early 1870s, and for a couple of years in the late 1880s steam trams were used on at least one route. Horse trams regained their monopoly in 1889, but ten years later electric trams were introduced to Plymouth's streets.
PHOTOGRAPH: JOHN SMITH

Mutley was a fairly upmarket area, although until the 1890s Mutley Plain still had the health hazard of an open water supply on its west side. This turn-of-the-century view looks north along Mutley Plain roughly from what was known as 'Lewis Jones Gate' - the point where, until the 1850s, road tolls were collected. This shopping centre and its counterpart at Devonport were the only ones in the Three Towns to survive World War II. The railway is nowhere to be seen - it runs through a tunnel under the church on the left.

it. The engine and a few of the carriages of the Cornwall train were also somewhat damaged in the first collision with the pilot engine'.

Five passengers sustained slight injuries as a result of the collisions. In his report, Colonel Yolland placed the blame on the engine shed switchman for having omitted to put his up distant signal at danger before giving the 'all clear' to the pilot engine. The Colonel pointedly observed that: '*The incident could not have occurred if the engine shed switchman had been provided with the proper signals, fitted with those mechanical appliances which are now almost universally adopted, to prevent signalmen from making mistakes that frequently lead to collisions through mere acts of forgetfulness*'.

The South Devon Railway was, of course, a broad gauge concern. The second broad gauge company to serve Plymouth was the Cornwall Railway which, on 4 May 1859, opened its line from Cornwall Junction (half a mile north of Millbay) to Truro for public passenger traffic. The Cornwall Railway's best-known feature in the Plymouth area was undoubtedly the Royal Albert Bridge, which carried the line across the River Tamar.

On the Plymouth side of the Tamar, the CR initially had only one station - Devonport (suffixed Albert Road on 26 September 1949) - but additional stations were opened by the GWR at Keyham (1 July 1900) and St.Budeaux (1 June 1904), and halts at Wingfield Villas (1 June 1904), Dockyard (1 June 1905), and Ford (1 June 1904). Of those extra stopping places, Wingfield Villas halt closed in June 1921 and Ford platform (after sustaining bomb damage) on 6 November 1941.

The additional halts were provided for railmotor services, introduced in the Plymouth area by the GWR in 1904. During 1905 ten railmotors were usually allocated to Laira for the services, but the units generated more local traffic than they could handle and were soon replaced by auto-trains. By 1910 only six railmotors remained at Plymouth, and by January 1914 the allocation was nil. Apart from

Mutley station, early 1900s. This view looks east towards the mouth of the 183yd-long tunnel under Mutley Plain. Mutley station - known as the 'gentrys' station' on account of its usually well-heeled clientele - had a comparatively short life, opening on 1 August 1871 and closing on 2 March 1939. Immediately before World War I the station had a staff of seventeen and was taking well over £20,000pa in fares; during the 1930s - its final years - it had a staff of seven but the annual receipts ultimately plummeted to only a little over £3,000. The photographic technique demonstrated here is interesting - the apparent 'compression' of the distance between the station and the tunnel indicates that some form of telephoto lens was used. PHOTOGRAPH: JOHN SMITH

Mutley station, July 1930. Having dashed up the 1 in 72 from Mutley Tunnel, a Churchward 2-6-0 approaches the station with a heavy westbound train. The engine is believed to be No.8393, one of sixty-five '5300' series Moguls which, in 1928, had their weights increased and redistributed in order to reduce flange wear. PHOTOGRAPH: F.H.C. CASBOURN, COURTESY R.C.RILEY

a couple of short-term allocations to Laira in 1929/30, the machines did not return to Plymouth.

Reverting to the ghoulish matter of accidents, on 15 April 1873 an incident occurred to the north of Devonport station on the Cornwall Railway - the 2am down goods train, a tank engine, fifteen loaded wagons and two brake

North Road Rates, 1906	SINGLE FARES			RETURN FARES		
TO	1st	2nd	Parly.	1st	2nd	Parly.
Plymstock	6d	4d	3d	9d	7d	n/a
Yealmpton	11d	10d	8d	1s8d	1s7d	n/a
Millbay	3d	2d	1d	4d	3d	n/a
Devonport (via Millbay)	4d	3d	2d	7d	5d	n/a
Saltash (via Millbay)	11d	7d	3d	1s5d	1s	n/a
Liskeard (via direct loop)	3s	2s	1s7d	5s6d	3s6d	n/a
Par (via direct loop)	5s9d	3s8d	2s10d	10s6d	6s6d	n/a
Penzance	13s6d	8s6d	6s8d	23s6d	14s9d	n/a

vans, with two guards, one (the 'head guard') riding in the van at the tail of the train, and the other in a van which was *supposed* to have been about sixth from the engine, left Plymouth at 4.39am. It passed Devonport station without stopping, and was travelling, according to the driver, at some 18 - 20 miles an hour. 'When the engine had got on the southern end of the high wooden viaduct, called the Camels-head, or Weston Mill Creek Viaduct' runs Colonel Yolland's Report, the driver said he *'felt a bit of a jerk behind and on looking back he found that he had lost the greater part of his train, having three trucks only still attached to his engine, the trailing wheels of the last truck being off the rails'.*

'The driver states that as soon as he found out something was wrong, he shut off steam, sounded

the break whistle, and stopped the engine at the northern end of the viaduct, which is 396 yards in length, with the rails about 40 feet above the level of the water; and when he had stopped he heard the head guard of the train calling out for him to go back. He says he left the engine in charge of his fireman, and walked back to the southern end of the viaduct, where he found the rest of his train, some on the rails, some on top of the embankment, some down the eastern side of the embankment, and others lying in the mud of the creek below. He assisted the head guard, and some other men who had got to the spot, in lifting a cask of whisky, which was lying on the legs and lower part of the body of the second guard of the train, at the bottom and at the east side of the embankment...'

That, however, was not the end of the episode. The 4.50am down mail train from Plymouth, hauled by a 4-4-0ST and comprising three carriages and two vans, was following on behind. After being given the 'all clear' at Devonport station at 5.0am, the down mail continued its journey and ploughed into the remains of the goods train. Fortunately, the mail had been slowed to about 10mph prior to impact, but even that speed was enough to wreck all fourteen of the goods wagons which had remained on the line, and also cause considerable damage to the viaduct.

In his report, Colonel Yolland explained that the line was worked with the assistance of the electric telegraph on the absolute block

system. When the telegraph post near the Camel's Head Viaduct, where the accident occurred, was knocked down and the wires broken, some wires fell into the water, 'earthing' and completing the electrical circuit between Devonport and the Camel's Head Viaduct. The result was that 'although the needle at Saltash' (the next station on the line - at the Cornish end of the Royal Albert Bridge) 'was pinned over to "train on line" for the down goods train by the Saltash signalman, the needle at Devonport (which could not be moved while the wire was intact to Saltash and the needle pinned over) became free and resumed the vertical position, when the wire broke and touched "earth"'. The 'policeman' (signalman) at Devonport 'not unnaturally concluded', being entirely ignorant of any accident to the goods, that it had reached Saltash station, and 'he fancied that the Saltash station signalman had forgotten to notify him when that train had reached that station. He tried to get "line clear" from Saltash for the down mail train, but was unable to get any reply; and he decided to send on the train; but unfortunately he did not caution the driver and tell him that he was unable to get "line clear" from Saltash, and that in consequence he must proceed cautiously'.

Miraculously, the only casualty in the accident was the second guard of the goods train, who sustained badly broken ribs. Colonel Yolland blamed the policeman at Devonport for the accident, and it seems that the Cornwall Railway had done likewise; the Colonel was unable to interview the policeman, 'as he no longer worked for the Company'.

The Cornwall Railway and the South Devon Railway were taken over by the GWR in February 1876. In May 1876 mixed gauge rails were laid between Lydford (on the Launceston branch) and Plymouth so that the London & South Western Railway could have access to

YEAR	TICKETS		RECEIPTS	PARCELS		TOTAL REC.	STAFF	
	Issued	Season		Number	Receipts		No.	Wages
1903	204,339	?	£36,070	16,195	£1,686	£37,756	31	£2,385
1913	246,245	?	£52,287	30,148	£2,583	£54,870	47	£3,837
1923	352,153	736	£136,364	46,489	£3,940	£140,304	71	£13,617
1929	321,890	425	£166,037	450,404	£44,323	£200,360	69	£16,214
1930	290,857	539	£157,306	547,398	£48,568	£205,874	71	£16,906
1931	270,940	765	£149,430	496,801	£36,313	£185,743	103	£17,831
1932	262,063	1,270	£137,160	509,257	£36,163	£173,323	105	£17,839
1933	245,469	3,464	£131,633	571,626	£37,679	£169,212	103	£18,050
1934	253,686	4,501	£135,333	685,497	£39,416	£174,749	104	£18,309
1935	247,457	4,767	£137,901	677,082	£22,206	£160,107	105	£19,294
1936	250,352	5,253	£162,529	596,966	£22,822	£175,411	110	£20,757
1937	268,139	5,702	£168,604	604,441	£23,129	£191,733	110	£21,771
1938	252,461	5,011	£174,367	608,907	£24,197	£198,564	115	£23,748

TABLE SHOWING PLYMOUTH NORTH ROAD PASSENGER TRAFFIC

Millbay station, 23 May 1892. The first up narrow gauge train departs from Millbay, the debris of the gauge conversion being clearly evident. The locomotive at the head of the train appears to be one of the convertible 0-4-4Ts (Nos.3541-3560), which had started life as 0-4-2STs and finished up as 4-4-0s. Should that be an incorrect locomotive identification, advice will no doubt be forthcoming - Plymouth's railway enthusiasts are very quick to identify errors. The wooden platform on the extreme left of the picture is the old ticket platform, which opened in August 1851. The working of incoming trains from the ticket platform didn't amuse the Board of Trade inspector, Colonel Yolland: '...the engines are there detached, run ahead, and are then shunted back out of the way, while a pilot engine comes out from the engine shed siding, crosses over the up main line and thence on to the down main line to the rear of the passenger train, which it then pushes forward from the ticket to the station platform'. The old goods depot is on the right of the picture, and the partly (mostly?) obscured track on its immediate left leads to the docks. The large building behind the station is the Duke of Cornwall Hotel, which opened in 1862.

the new station at North Road and, from there, to its own new terminus at Devonport. Predictably, the GWR's addition of standard gauge rails and the granting of running powers to the LSWR had not been conducted with obvious good grace.

At the time, Devonport was a more prosperous community than Plymouth, and so it served LSWR purposes well. Nevertheless, the company was keen to endorse its presence in Plymouth and, consequently, bided its time while the GWR slowly finished the new station

at North Road, which was intended for use by both the GWR and the LSWR. North Road station was inspected by Colonel Yolland on 1 March 1877: '*At the present time, there are up and down Platforms situated to the north of the up, and south of the down loop lines, and*

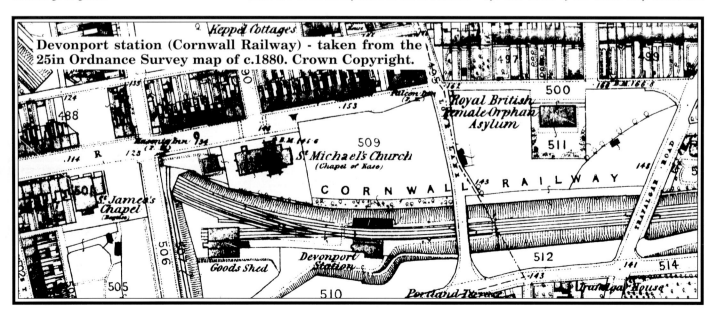

Devonport station (Cornwall Railway) - taken from the 25in Ordnance Survey map of c.1880. Crown Copyright.

Millbay station, 12 July 1955. Some summer sunshine, and even Millbay station could look almost inviting. After its closure to public passenger traffic in 1941 the station was used for goods and empty stock; here, 0-4-2T No.1434 heads the empty stock of the Tavistock auto train. In 1959 - just four years after this picture was taken - this view was no more, new carriage sidings having replaced the old passenger platforms. PHOTOGRAPH: R.C.RILEY.

provision has been made for the construction hereafter of two additional Platforms if required between those now constructed, and there are thus two main lines through the Station yard and two loop lines, which lie alongside of the present up and down platforms.

'Besides these lines there are various sidings east and west of the Station Buildings and Platforms.

'There are two Signal Boxes respectively at the eastern and western ends of the Station. The former contains 18 Levers of which 4 are spare ones, and the latter 23. At the eastern Signal Box an Electric Repeater is required for the down distant Signal, but in other respects the interlocking of the Points and Signals has been properly carried out. The lines are laid with mixed gauge.

'The Station is in an unfinished state. The up Platform is not yet all paved, nor the roof overhead covered in, and the Station Buildings including the Booking Office on the up Platform are mostly unfinished. The approach Road from the North Road to the up Platform remains to be made and fenced. The Sidings at the west end of the Station are being laid in at the present time. A clock is required to be placed so as to be seen from the Station Platforms. An over foot-bridge has been constructed to pass from one platform to the other.

'At the west end of the down Platform, a blind siding, entered by facing points, has been constructed, in continuation of the down loop line, not 100 yards in length, and abutting upon the North Road which passes under the Railway'.

The Colonel nevertheless recommended that, subject to removal of the blind siding on the down loop line, opening could be sanctioned. His caution about the siding stemmed largely from an accident at Tamworth (on the LNWR) in 1870 which had, it was agreed, been caused by facing points leading to a siding from a loop line - a similar arrangement to that at North Road.

The GWR and LSWR officers attending the inspection did not have the authority to make an immediate decision regarding the siding, and so a telegram was sent to the GWR at Paddington. The GWR hierarchy considered it advisable to discuss the matter internally, and Col. Yolland therefore had no option but to rescind the recommendation for opening. After deliberating over the matter of the troublesome siding, James Grierson of the GWR wrote to the Board of Trade on 6 March:

Millbay signal box, 1 May 1961. The hefty 'box was opened in 1914 to replace an older building a few yards to the north. It closed on 14 December 1969. PHOTOGRAPH R C RILEY.

Devonport (Albert Road) station, possibly early 1900s. This view looks west towards the tunnel; the signalbox beyond the platforms was taken out of use in November 1960, and the sidings (partly out of view behind the left-hand platform) were dispensed with between 1957 and 1964. The generous width between the platforms is, of course, a legacy of the broad gauge days.

'...*the object of putting in the Siding was to expedite the working of trains into Cornwall in order that, on the arrival of a train at the North Road Station, either the Cornwall or the Plymouth portion might be immediately disconnected, and also that an Engine could be standing in the Siding referred to, ready to take on the other portion of the train, so as to avoid delay, by simply backing on to it without shunting.*

'*If Col Yolland desires, the points leading from the Platform line for the Siding may be interlocked with the points leading from the main line into the loop line, in such a way that any train running into the platform line would, if it over-ran the platform, run out again on to the main line, and not into the Siding*'.

Col. Yolland countered by pointing out that North Road station was, at that time, required only by the LSWR (the GWR continuing to use Millbay for the time being), and opined that the LSWR could not have any use for the siding. He shrewdly remarked that he considered the GWR unjustified in keeping the LSWR out of the station by continuing to insist that the siding arrangement remain.

That suggestion of the GWR employing delaying tactics might not have been too wide of the mark. As stated by David St.John Thomas in Volume One of the *Regional History of the Railways of Great Britain*, it was originally intended that North Road station should have stone buildings, but the GWR was so tardy in building it that, for the sake of speed, timber had to be substituted. But we digress... The matter of the siding arrangement at North Road was not left in the hands of mere minions. Sir Daniel Gooch (the GWR chairman) met Sir Charles Adderly (the president of the Board of Trade), and it was agreed that, subject to all trains stopping at the platform and the siding being interlocked, opening would be sanctioned.

PLYMOUTH MILLBAY, passenger train traffic.

| Year | Tickets | | Receipts. | Parcels | | Total | Staff | |
	issued	season		No.	Rec.		No.	Wages
1903	390,671	?	£65,624	267,795	£28,808	£94,432	210	£17,203
1913	1,486,581	?	£109,010	421,511	£31,027	£140,037	201	£22,529
1923	900,584	1,845	£145,584	558,618	£59,175	£204,759	199	£45,363
1929	549,018	913	£130,637	269,337	£25,544	£156,181	267	£44,924
1930	474,359	765	£113,584	226,745	£23,115	£136,699	256	£43,424
1931	420,512	710	£93,283	239,505	£34,604	£127,887	228	£40,853
1932	399,823	827	£85,675	196,692	£22,382	£108,057	223	£39,098
1933	399,797	2,559	£82,907	174,367	£20,217	£103,124	223	£38,561
1934	410,302	3,365	£91,167	175,717	£19,910	£111,077	221	£38,379
1935	387,834	3,048	£94,406	175,551	£21,123	£115,529	234	£39,043
1936	366,789	3,216	£92,730	168,613	£20,529	£113,259	235	£43,418
1937	380,206	3,959	£104,730	164,051	£19,154	£123,884	238	£45,531
1938	328,559	3,218	£94,038	179,338	£22,570	£116,608	237	£46,847

Top left:- Weston Mill Viaduct, 1902/03. The Cornwall Railway's main line between Plymouth and Truro incorporated no less than thirty-four viaducts which, between them, had a total length of four miles. On the Plymouth side of the Tamar alone, there were three viaducts. The Cornwall Railway's viaducts were designed by Brunel who, somewhat fortunately for all concerned, had replaced Capt. W.S. Moorsom as the CR's engineer. Partly due to the CR's precarious finances, the viaducts were built largely of timber - American white pine, perversely known in this country as 'yellow pine'. Most of the CR's viaducts had, in Brunel style, timber superstructures on masonry piers, but a number of viaducts across creeks (where the mud was sometimes up to 70ft deep) had, of necessity, timber piers - 'miracles of struts and braces', as they were once described. One of the all-timber viaducts was at Weston Mill, two miles out from Cornwall Junction; it had thirty spans, was 400yd long, and carried the railway 46ft above the high-water mark. It was one of the last timber viaducts to remain on the CR line, its replacement - a structure of four steel spans flanked at each end by three brick and masonry arches - being completed in 1903. Needless to say, this picture shows the replacement viaduct under construction. Should the course of the creek under the viaduct seem odd, it should be explained that much of the land under the central section of the viaduct has since been reclaimed and built on.

Below:- Royal Albert Bridge, 1858. This superb photograph was, presumably, taken as an official record picture. The Royal Albert Bridge was only the third - but the last - suspension bridge to be built in this country for main line railway use. The first was designed by Capt. Samuel Brown to carry the Stockton & Darlington Railway across the River Tees; completed in 1830, it was so poorly executed that, almost from the outset, it had to be shored up with timber piles. It was replaced by a girder bridge in 1841. The second main line suspension bridge was Brunel's structure across the River Wye at Chepstow. Opened to traffic in 1852, it provided useful experience for the design of the Royal Albert Bridge. However, with the rebuilding of the Wye Bridge in 1962, the Royal Albert Bridge has, for the last thirty-odd years, been the only suspension bridge in the world to carry a main line railway. It was named after HRH The Prince Consort, who officiated at the opening ceremony on 3 May 1859. Sadly, Brunel was unable to be present at the opening - he was convalescing at Cairo, the stress of a lifetime's work having caught up with him. He died on 15 September at the age of just fifty-three, the Royal Albert Bridge therefore becoming the last of the great man's works to be completed in his life-time. The bridge and its environs were given the Rev. Williams cause for celebration in 'Our Iron Roads':
'...one of the most remarkable in the world ...the noble Tamar river, as its waters approach the little village of Saltash, narrows, and soon afterwards widens out into as fine a sheet of water as any of its kind in the kingdom, its distant banks decked with cottages and fringed with undulating woodlands down to the water's edge. Across this narrow part of the channel the viaduct hangs high in the air ...its height from foundation to summit is no less than 260 feet, or 50 feet higher than the summit of the Monument in London ...six inches have been allowed for expansion and contraction to each tube, but the greatest difference yet observed between the hottest and the coldest day has only made a difference of two inches in the length of the bridge'.

Bottom left:- Royal Albert Bridge, 1858. The Cornwall Railway might have been a poorly-financed concern, but it certainly had some pretty impressive engineering works. Its best-known legacy is undoubtedly the Royal Albert Bridge across the River Tamar. Much has been written elsewhere about the bridge, and so it seems a mite superfluous to repeat anything but the barest background details here. The bridge was, of course, designed by Brunel, although his original plan for taking the railway across the Tamar was a structure comprising one span of 225ft and six of 105ft, with a clearance of 80ft above high water. That proposal failed to find favour with the Admiralty as certain minimum clearances had to be observed, and so Brunel substituted a plan for a bridge consisting of two spans of 300ft and two of 200ft, which provided a clear headway of 100ft. This satisfied the Admiralty's requirements, but the cost of building a bridge with three piers in deep water did not amuse the Cornwall Railway's accountants. It was back to the drawing board. The final plan was for a bridge with only one pier in deep water and two spans each of 465ft (later reduced to 455ft), the decking being suspended from massive arched tubes - a 'combination of an arch and a suspension bridge, half the weight being placed on one and half on the other'. After the base of the river pier had been constructed - a major achievement in itself, not least because of the 70ft depth of the river at high tide - the trusses, which were built on the Devon shore, were floated into position on the ebb tide, allowed to rest on the piers, and subsequently raised by 3ft at a time by hydraulic jacks at either end while the piers were built up under them. Brunel had, in fact, gained valuable experience of the 'float and raise' procedure during the construction of Stephenson's tubular bridge across the Menai Straits. This magnificent picture shows the western truss of the Royal Albert Bridge in position and the eastern one ready for raising.

Royal Albert Bridge, possibly early 1900s. The bridge consumed 2,650 tons of wrought iron, 1,200 tons of cast iron, 459,000 tons of masonry and 14,000 cubic feet of timber. It cost £225,000 to build, a considerable saving having been made by providing for only a single track. The section across the bridge is, in fact, the only part of the entire Paddington - Penzance line which has never been double track. The cost of the Royal Albert Bridge has often been compared to that of the Britannia Tubular Bridge, which was designed by Robert Stephenson and opened in 1850. The Royal Albert Bridge was some 300ft longer than the Britannia Bridge and, significantly, didn't have the latter's advantage of a conveniently-placed rock on which the central pier could be founded, yet the Royal Albert Bridge cost £375,000 less to construct. In this picture, the alignment of the PDSWJR's Lydford - Plymouth line is discernible on the far bank, and so the picture must be post-1890. It has been suggested that the imposing paddle steamer in the picture might have been laid up for the winter, or is awaiting admission to a yard for repairs. It was probably used for cruising in the Channel, and although it could have navigated the Tamar, its length would have presented problems with turning.

Above & right:- Royal Albert Bridge, 22 July 1928. The bridge required little more than routine maintenance until 1903, when new steel girders were installed. In 1928 - when the structure was almost seventy years old - the plate girders of the approach spans were renewed and, in 1930, wind bracing was added. These pictures were taken during the renewal of the girders. One item of interest is the inscription on the girder - the Fairfield company of Chepstow was a descendant of Messrs. Finch & Willey, the very company which had constructed the Wye Bridge to Brunel's design. Note also the engineer's temporary siding, on which the train is standing.

The GWR requested official permission as soon as possible, James Grierson writing that the South Western 'was very anxious' to open the station, and the GW was 'desirous of giving every facility to do so...'.

Permission to open North Road was formally granted on 20 March 1877. It was not the most luxurious of stations, and as the GWR and LSWR traffic in the Plymouth area grew, it became increasingly cramped. At many places throughout the GWR network, the demise of the broad gauge in 1892 provided much-needed space for the rebuilding or enlargement of stations, and North Road was no exception. For the record, the last broad gauge engine to leave Plymouth was 'Standard Goods' 0-6-0 *Europa*, which started its journey to the scrap sidings at Swindon at 4am on Saturday 21 May.

At North Road, improvements were put in hand in the early 1900s. The finished job was inspected for the Board of Trade on 24 November 1908 - the work comprised the construction of two additional platforms, the lengthening of the existing up platform at the east end, the re-arrangement of the connections at each end of the station, two new signal boxes (one at each end of the station) and the 're-signalling of the whole place.' The new platforms were 600 and 750 feet long, reached by stairways from the existing footbridge. 'Complete waiting accommodation', including Ladies Room and 'conveniences for both sexes', were available on both new platforms. The new boxes were North Road East (40 levers in use and 8 spare) and North Road West with 39 levers in use and 20 spare.

To further assist the traffic flow, in 1913 a 65ft turntable was provided near Cornwall Junction (where the Millbay line diverged), and new connections were laid. The turntable at Plymouth Millbay had been only 45ft in diameter and so large engines requiring to turn had 'either to run to Laira or round the Cornwall Junction triangle', to considerable occupation of the main line in a very congested area - 'a very inconvenient and expensive arrangement'.

The works, which had initially been estimated at £3,555 (excluding the cost of the turntable), were inspected by Lt-Col von Donop on 15 September 1913. Mercifully for those of us who have sampled the Colonel's eccentric handwriting, the report was typed:

'(1) On the down side of North Road Station a new double junction, with facing connection on the down line, has been laid in on the Cornwall

Royal Albert Bridge, 13 December 1927.

loop lines; both new lines lead to the new turntable.

'The points and signals are worked from the existing North Road West Signal-box, which contains a frame of 49 working and 10 spare levers.

(2) On the up side of Cornwall Junction a new facing connection has been added on the up line to North Road, leading to the turntable road, and a new cross-over road has been constructed between the up and down lines.

'The points and signals are worked from the existing Cornwall Junction Signal-box, which contains a frame of 38 working levers and 1 spare lever.

'The only requirement noted was at Cornwall Junction, where, owing to the distance of the splitting signals from the new facing connection, the provision of an intermediate clearance bar is desirable, and this Company (the GWR) has agreed to provide'.

It was not only the movement of trains, but also the movement of passengers which was of more or less permanent concern. On 24 February 1916 the Divisional Superintendent at Plymouth wrote to Paddington on the subject of the North Road booking office - the station was a 'closed one and 'some difficulty' was experienced by passengers for up line destinations, coming to North Road by way of the down platform. It was on the town side of the station and they had to pass the collector at the door and go over the footbridge to the up side Booking Office in order to obtain tickets. With a view to minimising this it was arranged that tickets for those up line stations most frequently applied for should be provided in the down booking office, 'so that passengers may obtain such tickets at that Office before they come on to the platform'. The North Road station master was instructed to introduce tickets for certain down stations in the up Booking Office 'so that they might be issued to passengers who reach the station on the up side and who have to cross over the footbridge to the opposite side of the station to join down trains'.

It was not only GWR and LSWR engines which were seen at North Road. On 28 October 1904 a Great Central excursion from Lancashire was worked throughout by Robinson 4-4-2 No 267, an event which must have astonished those versed in such matters. The train, which carried passengers from Oldham, Stalybridge, Leeds, Hull and Manchester, had left London Road in Manchester at 11.30pm, and had travelled via Leicester, Banbury, Oxford, Bath and Bristol. It comprised five GCR bogies (141 tons tare) and a pair of GWR bogies which had been added at Exeter. The excursion arrived in Plymouth at 9.50am (on 29 October), left at 12.03am the following morning, and arrived back at Manchester at 9.50am. The round trip covered some 750 miles. Further Manchester - Plymouth excursions were operated in the following years, but it is thought that the pattern was different. During the Easter period of 1905 the GCR locomotive (No 265) was apparently taken off at Leicester, while another excursion later that year (with No 267 in charge again) seems to have switched to GWR power at Bristol.

Royal Albert Bridge, 16 July 1953. An auto train, being propelled towards Plymouth, passes Royal Albert Bridge box, which replaced an older box in 1908 but was itself closed in 1973. PHOTOGRAPH: E.R. MORTEN

Left:- Plympton, circa 1905/06: Although Plympton is a little beyond the geographical remit of this book, it is a convenient setting for GWR steam railmotor No.7. The Plymouth railmotors usually worked to and from Saltash, Yealmpton, Plymstock and Tavistock, but they created a demand with which it was impossible to cope, and were replaced by auto trains. The Plympton auto (one service each day - the 8.0am to Saltash) survived until June 1959, when Plympton station closed to passengers - the buses, which operated a ten-minute interval service, had taken most of the local traffic. As for the old steam railmotors, the coach sections of most were ultimately converted to auto trailers; a few remained in service until the late 1950s, while some in departmental stock survived until the mid-1960s.

Table 4 PLYMOUTH MILLBAY GOODS

Year	Forwarded (tons)			Received (tons)			coal/coke not charged	Total		Livestock vans	Staff	
	coal/coke	minerals	general	coal/coke	minerals	general		tons	receipts		No.	wages
1903	12,441	29,476	113,173	1,712	28,333	53,916	302	239,353	£117,289	1,457	?	?
1913	21,869	1,380	143,433	1,140	86,423	70,004	4,764	329,013	£145,876	790	110	£8,869
1923	1,461	4,796	122,162	5,843	13,164	75,845	14,436	237,707	£253,090	69	151	£25,305
1929	19,588	2,618	103,312	886	19,908	78,015	4,497	228,824	£253,374	43	148	£25,714
1930	24,845	4,578	133,438	2,277	16,060	86,234	6,765	274,197	£279,052	178	150	£25,567
1931	83,430	14,762	169,687	7,736	30,545	124,815	15,935	446,910	£387,783	1,262	183	£30,258
1932	78,027	15,895	156,256	6,346	21,047	113,808	16,241	407,620	£346,947	1,401	172	£28,176
1933	64,749	16,021	138,732	7,483	23,234	113,842	22,365	386,426	£329,425	1,187	172	£28,357
1934	63,850	15,300	146,953	6,493	24,391	114,323	23,010	394,320	£340,134	1,094	173	£29,282
1935	63,168	18,911	135,831	6,916	19,983	120,737	27,753	393,379	£346,837	919	179	£29,882
1936	53,832	18,452	134,061	6,375	21,835	115,507	26,976	377,038	£350,854	857	181	£30,834
1937	45,131	27,147	117,400	6,701	24,541	118,973	22,437	362,330	£358,517	815	182	£31,765
1938	36,663	16,211	97,178	1,458	27,557	118,282	18,870	316,219	£357,483	670	186	£34,202

1938 paybill includes £1,160 for 'show expenses'. From 1931, figures include Laira, Devonport and Sutton Harbour Goods

Above:- North Road station, 1910. Opened in 1877 for use by the GWR and LSWR, North Road became Plymouth's main station. The removal of the broad gauge rails in 1892 provided some space for much-needed improvements, and by 1908 the two existing platforms had been lengthened and two additional platforms constructed. This picture was taken about eighteen months after the completion of the works.

In later years, another notable visitor to Plymouth was SR 'Lord Nelson' No 859 LORD HOOD - believed to be the only SR 4-6-0 to reach Plymouth. It made the trip in 1934, its journey from Exeter being via Newton Abbot (the GWR route), and was exhibited at Devonport station.

North Road station gained more prominence after the 'Three Towns' - Devonport, Stonehouse and Plymouth - effectively became one in 1914, but the original terminus at Millbay was not completely forgotten. In 1899 Millbay was resignalled and a new box constructed, Col. Yorke making a preliminary inspection for the Board of Trade on 10 July. His only suggestion was that, as the lines leading to and from the docks were occasionally used for passenger trains, facing point locks should be provided at either end of a cross-over road, which formed the access to and outlet from these lines. The final inspection of the completed works at Millbay was made on 14 July 1903 by Lt-Col. von Donop who, frustratingly for those of us with no knowledge of hieroglyphics, chose to write his report by hand... The lines had been rearranged and new platforms provided, giving two islands each about 500ft long, 3 ft high 'and of ample width'. Four platform lines were put in, on each side of these island platforms.

North Road station, 1939. Despite having been enlarged in 1908, by the 1930s North Road station was again in dire need of extensive upgrading. This started in 1938, but was interrupted by the war and did not resume until 1956. Nevertheless, this picture reveals that, by 1939, work on the new platforms on the north side of the station was well in hand.

Below:- The GWR issued a series of books entitled 'Through the Window', each one charting the scenic and historical delights of a particular main line. This page is an extract from the 1939 edition of the Paddington - Penzance book.

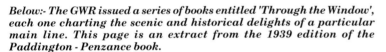

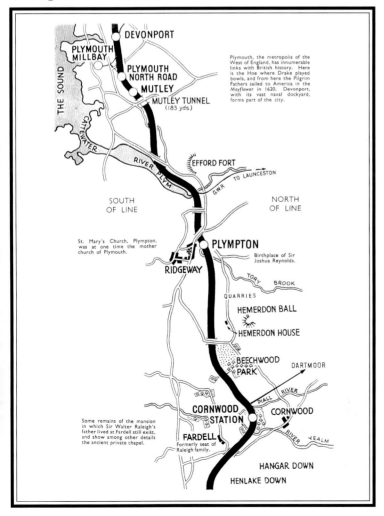

Despite the improvements to Millbay station, from the 1920s an increasing number of GWR services terminated at North Road. The shortness of the platforms at Millbay was the major problem, and many Cornish expresses were eventually routed via the Cornwall Junction 'loop' (opened in May 1876), thereby missing Millbay completely. Nevertheless, by the late 1930s Millbay was still handling a greater volume of passenger traffic than North Road station, although the latter's traffic produced more revenue.

After the alterations to Millbay at the turn of the century, the station received very little investment, and in later years it looked as if it owed its origins to the 'art desperate' school of architecture. Millbay station was closed to passengers on 23 April 1941 - the adjoining goods station had suffered bomb damage, and the passenger platforms were required for goods. The loss of Millbay passenger facilities was a major inconvenience to operations in the Plymouth area, for although the rebuilding of North Road had started in 1938, the outbreak of war delayed further progress, work not recommencing until 1956.

Above:- North Road station, 1939. Although the improvement works to the inside of the station commenced in 1938, the concourse had to wait until the 1950s before being modernised. By then, the station was likened to a 'shabby country junction'. The civil engineer's yard was behind the hoardings on the left. The taxis (on the left of the concourse) will undoubtedly be of interest to car enthusiasts. Note the uniformed cabbies. The Brooke Bond Tea van - wasn't there a Dinky Toy of such a vehicle?

Left:- North Road station, 27 August 1951. This picture shows very clearly - painfully, even - just how badly Plymouth's premier main line station required modernisation. These facilities hardly befitted a major city in the 1950s, especially one which had, of tragic necessity, to be almost completely rebuilt. PHOTOGRAPH: JOHN SMITH

Below:- North Road station, 1924. The passengers and mails from the R.M.S.MAURETANIA are hauled non-stop through North Road on their journey from Millbay Docks to Paddington. The GWR's publicity machine proudly announced that the 227-mile trip took only 243 minutes, and that 'the train was drawn by one of the GWR's new "Castle" class of engine, and a speed of over 80 miles an hour was attained in the course of the journey'. PHOTOGRAPH: BY ARRANGEMENT JOHN TATCHELL

Right:- North Road station, 2 June 1922. For many years the double-framed 'Dukes' and their successors, the 'Bulldogs', were synonymous with the West of England, but they were gradually displaced by Churchward '43XX' Moguls and, later, mixed traffic 4-6-0s. No.3283 COMET was one of the longer-lived 'Dukes', not being withdrawn until December 1950; a Plymouth engine at the time this picture was taken, it was probably engaged on carriage shunting duties. PHOTOGRAPH: H.C. CASSERLEY

Apart from the branch to Launceston, which left the main line at Tavistock Junction (two and three quarter miles east of North Road station), the only other GWR branches in the Plymouth area were to Sutton Harbour and Yealmpton. The former was a goods-only line, the alignment of which had been inherited from the 4ft 6in Plymouth & Dartmoor Railway. It was relaid with broad gauge rails and reopened for horse-worked traffic in May 1853, but despite being upgraded (on a slightly modified alignment) for locomotives in 1856/57, it did not accommodate them until 19 April 1869.

The Yealmpton branch was opened in 1898, an account of the opening appearing in the February issue of *The Railway Magazine* that year: '*On Saturday January 15th, The Countess of Morley opened for traffic a new line of railway from Plymstock to Yealmpton, a distance of six and a half miles, the total distance from Plymouth (Millbay Station) to Yealmpton being nine and a half miles.*

'*A double loop has also been constructed at Laira to give direct access between the Great Western main line and the Plymstock and Yealmpton branch.*

'*A special train of first-class saloon carriages left Millbay at noon on Saturday for Yealmpton. Quite appropriately the train was drawn by an engine named "Lady Morley", and gaily decorated with evergreens and flowers, and a trophy of flags in front*'.

The subject of GWR motive power in Plymouth has been well documented elsewhere. Suffice it to say that the main line from Paddington was usually treated to Swindon's finest - from the 1890s the outside-framed 4-4-0s held sway, then the 'Saint' 4-6-0s and their 4-4-2 alternatives, followed by the four-cylinder 'Stars' and, from the 1920s, the 'Castles' and

Top:- *North Road station, 9 August 1924. As with other pre-Churchward 0-6-0 tank engines, the '850' class started life with saddle tanks but later received pannier tanks. No.1905 was built in 1881, fitted with panniers in 1926, and withdrawn in 1936. It spent much of its later life in the West Country - usually at Plymouth, Exeter or Taunton. PHOTOGRAPH: F.H.C. CASBOURN, COURTESY R.C. RILEY*

Middle:- *North Road station, 24 April 1925. During the exchange trials of 1925, two LNER 'A1s' were pitted against two GWR 'Castles' - one of each type on LNER metals and the other pair on the GWR. The LNER engine dispatched to the GWR was No.4474, which had yet to receive its name of VICTOR WILD. During the week of the trials, the 'A1' worked the 10.30am Paddington - Plymouth on Monday, Wednesday and Friday and returned with the following days' 12.30pm Plymouth - Paddington. Those trains were worked on the alternate days by the GWR's representative, No.4074 CALDICOT CASTLE. This splendid picture shows the 'A1' running light from North Road to Laira shed. PHOTOGRAPH: F.H.C. CASBOURN, COURTESY R.C. RILEY*

Left:- *North Road station, 10 August 1925, with well-groomed 'County' 4-4-0 No.3835 COUNTY OF DEVON. PHOTOGRAPH: F.H.C. CASBOURN, COURTESY R.C. RILEY*

North Road station, 26 July 1924. No.4006 RED STAR leaves North Road light engine, bound, presumably, for Laira. This engine was one of the first 'Stars' to be withdrawn, retirement coming in November 1932. PHOTOGRAPH: F.H.C. CASBOURN, COURTESY R.C. RILEY

'Kings'. Between 1904 and 1927, the GWR's Paddington - Plymouth service was the longest non-stop working in the world. It also saw some of the best rolling stock. In 1931 the GWR decided to build eight 'super saloons' for the route, the first two being named *King George* and *Queen Mary*. The were 'the acme of luxurious travelling for railway passengers' fully worthy of their names. The interior decorations were beautifully carried out, the saloons and coupe compartments, as the *GWR Magazine* lovingly recounted, 'panelled in highly polished natural light French walnut veneer, with dark figured burr walnut pilasters on panels between the windows'.

For the GWR Centenary year of 1935 the long-established '10.30 Limited' train was formally retitled the 'Cornish Riviera Limited', and new rolling stock (appropriately known as 'Centenary Riviera stock') was built specially. The coaches were 60ft long and 9ft 7in wide. A train of thirteen 'Centenary' coaches weighed 420 tons tare, and could seat 84 first- and 336 second-class passengers, with dining car accommodation for a further 88. The fly in the ointment was that, due to the width of the vehicles, they were given a 'Red Triangle' restriction effectively limiting them to the old broad gauge routes. They were withdrawn from

Left:- Laira, 4 July 1957. In 1935 - the GWR's Centenary year - the title of 'Cornish Riviera Limited' was formally bestowed on the long-established '10.30 Limited'. The 'Riviera' was advertised to run non-stop between Paddington and Plymouth, although there was a pause at Newton Abbot for the assisting engine to be attached or detached. That said, where might the pilot engine be in this picture? It's summertime, and so the loading of the train would almost certainly have been around 400 tons - although Kings had demonstrated their ability to haul such a load unaided over the South Devon banks, the official restriction for the class was 360 tons. The locomotive here is No.6019 KING HENRY V, and the train is passing the site of Laira halt, which closed in July 1930. PHOTOGRAPH: R.C. RILEY

Laira Halt, 4 July 1957. Having brought the 'Riviera' into Plymouth, No.6019 KING HENRY V runs light through the disused up platform of Laira Halt on its way to Laira shed. PHOTOGRAPH: R.C. RILEY

Above:- Laira Yard, probably late 1920s. Among the many fascinating aspects of Plymouth's railway history are the Plymouth & Dartmoor Railway and the Lee Moor Tramway. The P&D, a 4ft 6in gauge horse-worked line, opened between Princetown and Sutton Harbour in 1823. The Lee Moor Tramway - also 4ft 6in gauge and horse-worked - opened between Lee Moor and the P&DR's Cann Quarry branch in 1854. The LMT was intended as an export route for the china clay and gravel from the Lee Moor area (to the north east of Plymouth on the edge of Dartmoor), the goods being transported via the P&DR to Laira Wharves (better known as Martins Wharf) at Cattewater Harbour. The histories of the LMT and P&DR are closely intertwined, but whereas the former eventually graduated to locomotive haulage on the upper part of its route, the latter remained horse-worked throughout. The P&DR - or, rather, what was left of it - passed to the Southern Railway at the grouping. By then, the only operational sections of the P&DR were, in effect, those used by the LMT. The LMT continued to dispatch goods in horse-drawn trains although, inevitably, the traffic passing over the old P&DR to Martins Wharf decreased over the years. Traffic all but ceased during World War II, resuming only intermittently after the war. The upper section of the tramway closed in 1947, as did the southern extremity beyond Maddock's Concrete Works adjacent to Friary Junction, and from then on the traffic was very sporadic. It was, however, not until October 1960 when the last section of the LMT/P&DR closed for good, much of the intermittent traffic during the final years having been primarily to preserve the status of a right of way. The LMT/P&DR passed by the east side of Laira yard - here a train of empties, presumably from Martins Wharf, being hauled northwards past the GWR sidings towards Marsh Mills. PHOTOGRAPH: F.H.C. CASBOURN, COURTESY R.C. RILEY

'Riviera' service in 1941, and after the war were put to use on a variety of other services.

The GWR was also active in other fields of transport. On 12 September 1904 the company introduced a motor-bus service between Plymouth, Crown Hill and Roborough, a total distance of six miles. Whether coincidence or not, Roborough was the home of Sir Massey Lopes, one of the GWR's most influential directors (and an M.P. to boot). Somewhat more spectacular than the bus service was the introduction, in May 1933, of a daily air service between Birmingham, Cardiff and Plymouth, the aeroplanes using Roborough Aerodrome to the north of Plymouth. The services were operated in conjunction with Imperial Airways, with a three-engined Westland Wessex six-seater for what was Britain's first railway-operated air service. The fares between Plymouth and Birmingham (including transfers to and from the main line stations) in 1933 were £5.10s.0d return and £3 single, but for the summer of 1934 the return fare was reduced to £4.10s.0d, while the Plymouth - Cardiff fare was £3.5s.0d return and £2.2s.0d single.

Left:- Laira Yard, probably late 1920s. At the north-east extremity of Laira Yard, there was an exchange siding for the transfer of traffic from the Lee Moor Tramway. The yard and, inevitably, the exchange siding were closed at the end of 1958 in preparation for the extensive remodelling of the railways at Laira. PHOTOGRAPH: F.H.C. CASBOURN, COURTESY R.C. RILEY

Left:- Between Mount Gould Junction and Friary Junction, probably late 1920s. A train of wagons heads south on the P&DR/LMT, bound for either Maddock's Concrete Works or Martins Wharf. PHOTOGRAPH: F.H.C. CASBOURN, COURTESY R.C.RILEY

Below:- Laira Junction, 16 July 1953. An 0-6-0PT, possibly No.6419 (which was indeed a Laira engine throughout the year), heads east across the Lee Moor Tramway crossing with what is almost certainly a Tavistock branch train. The auto trailer sidings on the right of the train are surprisingly full for a weekday (this was a Thursday). Was there some problem with auto workings? PHOTOGRAPH: E.R. MORTEN

Above:- Near Plymstock, 20 August 1951. Still waiting to have its smokebox numberplate applied, '57XX' 0-6-0PT No.8709 approaches Plymstock with the Yealmpton branch goods. PHOTOGRAPH: ALAN LATHEY

Below:- Billacombe, 17 March 1958. The Yealmpton branch lost its passenger services once and for all in October 1947, but goods services continued until the end of February 1960. The branch goods, in the charge of 0-6-0PT No.9716, shunts at Billacombe. PHOTOGRAPH: HUGH DAVIES

The Park, Devonport. W 1691.

Until the amalgamation of the 'Three Towns' (Devonport, Plymouth and Stonehouse) in 1914, Devonport was considered the most upmarket of the three. It nevertheless comprised quite a cross-section of housing - from impressive 'des res' villas to terraced accommodation for the numerous dockyard workers. The dockyard connection at Devonport was inescapable, but the town's impressive park - which was laid out from 1858 - was actually built on land obtained from the Army. Unfortunately, the dockyard made Devonport a prime target during the war, and in April 1941 much of the town was flattened by enemy bombs, some 17,500 properties being destroyed or damaged. In the early days of the railways, Devonport offered the LSWR satisfactory scope for custom, this photograph of the seemingly prosperous town (taken from the 'top' or Stoke end of the park) probably being taken circa 1900.

Chapter Two
The LSWR and the Southern
'... free and equal access for narrow gauge traffic...'

The London & South Western Railway was behind various schemes of the early 1850s which proposed a standard gauge route to Plymouth. It was, however, the LSWR's arrival at Exeter in 1860 which, arguably, provided the spur for renewed (and re-invigorated) efforts to reach Plymouth. Inevitably, the LSWR encountered considerable opposition from the broad gauge companies, though the 'narrow' gauge lobby was well supported in Plymouth itself, and also had useful backing in high places. A Commons Committee recommended: '....*that facilities should be afforded for the extension of the narrow-gauge between the Okehampton Railway at Lidford* (later known as Lydford) *and Plymouth, and that free and equal access for narrow-gauge traffic from Lidford into Plymouth and the Great Western Docks and Sutton Pool should be secured, together with sufficient station accommodation. The committee was also of opinion that additional accommodation is required for Devonport, and that the nar-row-gauge should be laid down in such a manner as to give direct access to the Dock-yards'.*

The squabbles that ensued between the LSWR and the broad gauge companies have been well documented elsewhere and, as this modest little book is not intended to be a complete history, it is not necessary to repeat the gory details here. Suffice it to say that the Okehampton - Lydford line opened on 12 October 1874. A connection was made at Lydford with the South Devon Railway's Plymouth - Launceston branch, and the LSWR invoked powers compelling the broad gauge South Devon to lay mixed gauge rails between Lydford and Plymouth, thereby giving LSWR trains access to the latter.

LSWR trains entered Plymouth from the east, passed through the uncompleted mixed gauge station at North Road, and then diverged southwards on to a new double track line which led to a purpose-built terminus at Devonport. The spur to Devonport, 54.2 chains in length and built

by the LSWR's thinly-veiled subsidiary, the Devon & Cornwall Railway, was inspected for the Board of Trade by Colonel Yolland on 1 March 1876; he reported that the only station on the line, Devonport, was provided with a turntable - the steepest gradient was 1 in 94.3, and the sharpest curve had a radius of nine chains. All bridges were substantially constructed, and the line was 'well finished and in good order', although the station buildings were unfinished. Because of this incompleteness, the Colonel declined to recommend that the station be opened; the necessary work was, however, soon finished, and LSWR trains started working into Plymouth and Devonport on 17 May 1876.

The SDR was far from amused by having been forced to provide a route for its rival. Its antagonism was such that it had to have its corporate arm twisted before reluctantly withdrawing an intention to charge the LSWR 'opening day' VIPs full fare for the ceremonial journey. The SDR got its own back on the return trip, the

No - not one of the LSWR's Ocean Liner tenders, but the Cremyll Ferry - the vessel seen here is loading for Mutton Cove at Devonport. The perhaps better-known Cremyll - Stonehouse ferry sailed from the hard around the corner off right. Mount Wise is in the distance, and the LSWR's Ocean Terminal is just out of view around the corner behind the warehouses (on the right of the frame, on the far side of the water).

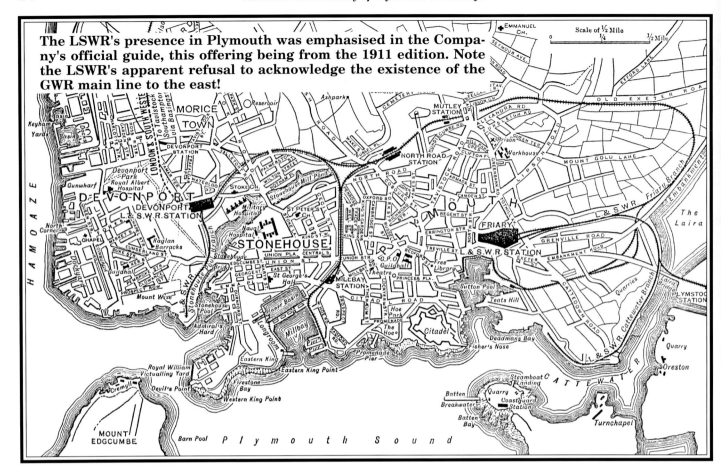

The LSWR's presence in Plymouth was emphasised in the Company's official guide, this offering being from the 1911 edition. Note the LSWR's apparent refusal to acknowledge the existence of the GWR main line to the east!

Exeter & Plymouth Gazette reporting that: '*the same courtesy was not, however, extended to the officials and others who returned in the evening ...and the full fare was exacted*'.

At the time, the siting of the LSWR terminus was a shrewd move, for Devonport was somewhat larger and rather more prosperous than Plymouth itself. The station reflected the up-market nature of the community it served, historian R.A. Williams pointing that it was designed by Galbraith, 'its light and graceful ironwork roofing from Belgium surmounting buildings of local limestone dressed with Portland stone'. An alternative, and somewhat less restrained description of the terminus was 'elegant, commodious and superior'. Devonport station was indeed smart. It had the luxury of an overall roof, although it survived only until 1941 when, bomb damaged, it was removed as a safety precaution. Before the rebuilding of North Road station recommenced in 1956, it was said that even the roofless Devonport (or Kings Road, as it had been suffixed in September 1949) made its neighbour look like a 'shabby country junction'.

The LSWR's euphoria at having reached Plymouth eventually gave way to a sense of frustration. Considerable delays became commonplace on the jointly-used single-track Lydford - Plymouth section, and the LSWR frequently complained that, when delays occurred, it was

their trains which were worst affected. The business community in Plymouth shared the LSWR's frustration, and the outcome was the incorporation in 1883 of the Plymouth, Devonport & South Western Junction Railway.

The PDSWJR proposed an independent double track line between Lydford and Plymouth, and although it was intended that the new line be used exclusively by the LSWR, it was formed and financed mainly by local businessmen. The 22.5

Devonport (LSWR) station, post-1890. Suffixed 'Kings Road' as from 26 September 1949, the LSWR's terminus had its end walls (on the right of the picture) pierced in 1890 to convert it into a through station. The premises were described as 'smart, commodious and superior' - a bit of a contrast to the GWR stations at Millbay and North Road. The elegant frontage seen here originally served the departure side, but after the conversion to a through station in 1890, the platform immediately behind this frontage accommodated down trains bound for North Road and Friary. The platform buildings (waiting rooms etc.) were, therefore, of comparatively little use to most passengers and, consequently, were under-used for most of the station's life. PHOTOGRAPH: JOHN SMITH

Devonport (LSWR) station, 30 August 1945. The station roof sustained bomb damage in 1941, and was subsequently removed as a safety precaution. This view looks towards St.Budeaux. PHOTOGRAPH: H.C. CASSERLEY

mile line from Lydford to Plymouth opened to public traffic on 2 June 1890, bringing the LSWR into the Plymouth area from the west (the previous route via the SDR/GWR Tavistock branch having entered from the east) and piercing the end walls of the original terminus at Devonport to convert it to a through station.

There had been a few minor hiccups during the alterations to Devonport station - on 8 February 1890 for instance,

the PDSWJR directors heard that the contractors had 'diverted the Devonport Station Road without any instructions from the Company's Engineers' and immediately resolved that 'the Town Clerk be informed'. A 'strong remonstrance' had been addressed to the hapless Contractors. The Town Clerk was hardly grateful, and on 12 April 1890 the PDSWJR board considered a letter from the Devonport Corporation complaining of the new boundary fence in the Brickfields at

the entrance of Devonport Station which 'they' (the Corporation) considered 'unsightly and unsuitable for so prominent a position'. On the new PDSWJR line into Devonport, the stopping places near the southern end of the route were at Ford, renamed Ford (Devon) in July 1922, and St.Budeaux, which was suffixed Victoria Road in September 1949. Additional halts were provided in 1906 for railmotor services.

The LSWR presence in Plymouth was emphasised on 1 July 1891 when the thirteen year-old goods station at Friary (once designated 'Friary Gardens' and, later, 'Friary Green') opened in its new guise as a passenger terminus. The Friary branch had been inspected for the Board of Trade by Major Marindin, whose report was dated 24 June:

'...a double line 72 chains in length, commencing at a junction with the Sutton Harbour Branch of the Great Western Railway, and terminating at Friary Station...

'Between Mutley Station and the new Friary Station, the trains will run first over a part of the Great Western main line, then over the Laira Branch and a new spur (inspected March 1891); then over a portion of the old Sutton Harbour Branch, passed for passenger traffic at the same time; and then over the new Friary Branch. 'For the greater proportion of its length the line is upon an embankment with an extreme height of 20 feet, but the portion next to the terminus is in cutting and excavation.

Devonport (LSWR) station. We've leapt ahead a little to 1 August 1964. Many stations showed evidence of extreme neglect in their final years, but Devonport (King's Road) gave the impression of being well cared-for until the end. This picture was taken just five weeks before the station closed to passengers. PHOTOGRAPH: S.C. NASH

The ex-LSWR presence at Devonport is shown in this 25in Ordnance Survey map of 1933. Crown Copyright.

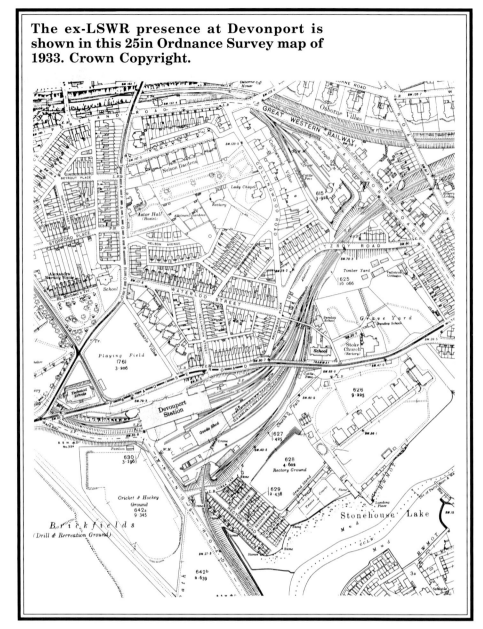

'There is one masonry over-bridge, with an arch of 43ft span, and two underbridges, one with a masonry arch of 10ft span, and the other with iron girders of 10ft span, which have sufficient theoretical strength.

'The station has four platforms and accommodation for passengers, and the platforms are covered for the greater proportion of their length. The signalling at the junction with the Sutton Harbour branch has already been inspected. There are two signal boxes at Friary Station, the Goods Yard box containing 41 working levers and 14 spare, and the Station box containing 37 working levers and 8 spare.'

Subject to certain requirements, the Major was happy to approve opening - various signalling rearrangements were necessary at the Station Box and the Goods Yard Box, 'the usual conveniences' should be provided in the ladies waiting room on the arrival platform, the approach roads required to be rolled and levelled and the labels on the different rooms still had to be fixed. A long siding at the junction was ordered 'continued and connected up with the Cattewater branch, so as to avoid any running of goods trains on the wrong line.'.

It appears that the LSWR had a virtually accident-free record in Plymouth in the nineteenth century. That said, there was a partial derailment on 6 April 1889 at Devonport Junction, where the LSWR joined the GWR about half a mile from Devonport (LSWR) station. No persons were hurt, but the Board of Trade recorded that the engine, Beattie 4-4-0 No 364, was 'slightly injured'.

In 1892, the LSWR constructed a branch between Friary and Plymstock, on the east bank of the River Plym, part of the line being laid on the route of the Plymouth & Dartmoor Railway. The P&DR was a 4ft 6in gauge horse-worked line - it had opened between King's Tor (near Princetown) and Sutton Harbour in Plymouth in 1823 and was later extended to Cattewater.

The inspection of the Plymstock branch was undertaken by Major Marindin, and

Left:- Devonport (Kings Road), 4 September 1951. Kings Road station was an interesting place, not least for the ferociously-graded line which passed underneath the goods shed en route to Stonehouse Pool. The station itself is visible on the right. The engine coasting down to Stonehouse Pool is 'O2' 0-4-4T No.30183. The station closed to passengers in September 1964, the signal box almost beneath the bridge was taken out of use in March 1965, and the goods facilities (and, finally, the Stonehouse Pool branch) closed in March 1971. This was one of the less-well photographed aspects of railway operations in Plymouth, most photographers mysteriously preferring the over-familiar 'art desperate' surroundings which prevailed at North Road station. PHOTOGRAPH: ALAN LATHEY

North Road station, 10 August 1925. The GWR station at North Road had, from the outset, been intended for use by the LSWR as well. Virtually all passenger services to and from the LSWR's Friary passed through North Road, the latter thereby becoming Plymouth's premier station, despite the presence of two exclusively-LSWR principal stations in the area. Here, 'T1' 0-4-4T No.74, still in pre-grouping plumage, approaches North Road with a St.Budeaux working. PHOTOGRAPH: F.H.C. CASBOURN, COURTESY R.C. RILEY

his first report concerned the section forming part of the Cattewater branch - it had been in use as a goods line for twelve years, and the junction with the LSWR main line into Friary Station had been rearranged and re-signalled. The portion inspected was single line, extending for 41 chains from the junction with the Friary line, which had been formed as a double junction, to an end on junction with 'Railway No.1 of the Plymouth & Dartmoor Railway Extension (1883), or the Laira Extension'.

Signalling at the junction was carried out from Friary Yard Cabin, which contained 55 working levers and controlled the points at the connection of the old piece of the Cattewater line, which remained a goods line, were worked from a ground frame locked by the train staff with which the line was to be worked.

Major Marindin's second report concerned the Laira extension of the Plymouth & Dartmoor Railway, which had also been a goods-only line. It commenced at an end-on junction with the Cattewater Branch of the LSWR, 'terminating for the present at Pomphlett, or as it is to be called, Plymstock Station'. The line was 52.27 chains long and single throughout, with a loop siding at the station.

The terminus at Pomphlett, or Plymstock, had only one platform, and the accommodation was described by Marindin as 'sufficient, although of a temporary character, as it is proposed to alter the position of the station when the line is extended further'. The usual minor adjustments were ordered - clock in the signal box, outside clock at the station, a thorough repainting of the 212 yard

iron viaduct over the Laira and 'an understanding to be given by the Plymouth & Dartmoor Company, and the LSWR (the working company) to work the line with one engine only in steam or two coupled together, carrying a staff'. Public traffic commenced on 5 September 1892.

An extension of the branch, on to Turnchapel, was opened on 1 January 1897, a goods-only spur continuing for ⅛-mile beyond the passenger station to a wharf on the river. Plymstock (alias 'Pomphlett') became a junction station on 17 January 1898 when the GWR branch to Yealmpton opened. The working instructions for the Turnchapel branch stipulated that the load of goods trains between Plymstock and Turnchapel Wharf must not exceed twelve loaded wagons and one van (ten wagons plus a van for Bayly's Siding) while the maximum for the Cattewater branch was sixty vehicles in the down direction and thirty plus one van in the up.

In October 1904 the LSWR transferred one of its two 'H12' steam railmotors to Plymouth for working the Turnchapel branch. The railmotors each had seating for eight first- and 32 third-class passengers, and had been built at a cost of £1,380 apiece specifically for working the newly-opened Basingstoke - Alton line. They

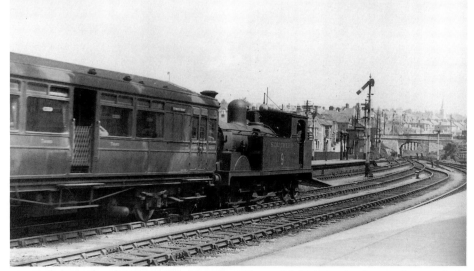

North Road station, 23 May 1935. A local working, with 'T1' No.9 in charge, departs from North Road. This engine was one of many which passed into BR ownership but was withdrawn without carrying its allotted number - in this case No.30009. PHOTOGRAPH: H.C. CASSERLEY

North Road station, probably 1939. A Friary - St.Budeaux local waits at North Road, with 'T1' 0-4-4T No.5 in charge. The engine was the last of the class to lose the cab roof brackets, pulleys and wire cables - components of the antiquated Drummond push-pull system - which were finally removed from No.5 in 1938. Although the engine survived until January 1950, in common with its classmates it failed to acquire its allotted BR number - in this instance 30005. PHOTOGRAPH: F.H.C. CASBOURN, COURTESY R.C. RILEY

had, however, proved wholly unsuitable for that duty, and had promptly been replaced by 'O2' 0-4-4Ts. Unit No 2 was subsequently subjected to trials in the Plymouth area, and after a short spell at Nine Elms Works for attention to its blast pipe, braking and lighting, returned to Plymouth for duties on the Turnchapel branch. It remained at Plymouth until February 1910, when it was transferred to Strawberry Hill for working the

Gunnersbury - Twickenham services. The unit was, incidentally, withdrawn in November 1916.

As for the railmotors themselves, a modified version of the 'H12s' was ordered in 1905. Classified 'H13', thirteen were built between October 1905 and June 1906. Unit No 7 was sent new to Plymouth in January 1906, and was joined later that year by No 8, formerly based at Guildford. With the 'H12' railmotor (No 2), they

were initially used on the Turnchapel branch but, from 26 September 1906, their sphere of operations was extended to St.Budeaux. The railmotors were successful enough for the LSWR Chief Mechanical Engineer (the ferocious Dugald Drummond) to order three larger units for use on the Tavistock run, but that order was later cancelled.

On 5 April 1905 - prior to the arrival of the 'H13' railmotors - the PDSWJR board had discussed a letter received from the LSWR general manager, Sir Charles Owens '...as to a Service of Motor Cars between Plymouth and Saltash'. The board resolved to provide a halt at Camels Head Bridge, albeit without a waiting room, but deferred on the subject of a halt between the two tunnels on the approach to Devonport. The latter (Albert Road halt) was later approved, and opened on 1 October 1906. Camels Head and Weston Mill halts opened on 1 November. The three halts did not have particularly long lives - Weston Mill closed on 27 June 1921, Camels Head on 4 May 1942, and Albert Road on 13 January 1947.

The LSWR railmotor services also used Lipson Vale halt and Mount Gould & Tothill halt, both of which were GWR property. The former - opened on 1 June 1904 - was between Mutley station and Laira, the latter - opened in October 1905 - near Friary Junction on the Plymstock line. Mount Gould & Tothill halt survived only until 1 February 1918. Lipson Vale

North Road station, 31 July 1946. Bullied Pacific No.21C115 (later 34015) EXMOUTH pulls away from North Road with the 3.45pm Friary - Waterloo. The Pacifics made their debut on the Exeter - Plymouth section in October 1945, and four were usually allocated to Friary shed until 1958. PHOTOGRAPH: S.C. NASH

North Road East, 6 September 1951. Some seven months before having its BR lined black livery applied, 'T9' No.30712 (an Exmouth Junction engine from February 1951 until November 1958) enters North Road with the 2.25pm Friary - Waterloo train. The engineer's siding on the right accommodates a neglected clerestory coach. PHOTOGRAPH: ALAN LATHEY

halt was closed on 22 March 1942 after its wooden platforms had been declared a safety hazard; since the cessation of the GWR suburban services in July 1930, it had been used only by the SR.

The LSWR's small fleet of railmotors were, to an extent, victims of their own success. They were considerably cheaper to operate than conventional trains and increased the traffic figures on several routes, but they could not have additional vehicles attached to accommodate the extra passengers. That said, two of the 'H13' units (*not* the Plymouth-based ones) had vestibules attached but there appears to

be no record of them ever running with trailer cars. A further annoyance with the railmotors was that, if one needed an overhaul, its entire carriage section was also put out of action. Even routine maintenance presented a problem as, when this was undertaken in the running sheds, the coach bodies became covered in grime.

Of Plymouth's 'H13' railmotors, No 7 was transferred to Guildford early in 1907 and No 8 went to Strawberry Hill in January 1910. The Working Timetable (WTT) for the summer of 1909 - when 'H12' No 2 and 'H13' No 8 were still active at Ply-

mouth - showed 20 down and 21 up passenger services on the Turnchapel branch each weekday plus one in each direction between Friary and Plymstock. Interestingly, the same WTT listed eight down and nine up passenger workings on the Great Western Yealmpton branch, while three LSWR and one GWR goods workings (as required) in each direction called at Plymstock on weekdays. Up to 66 trains were therefore handled at Plymstock each weekday and, apparently, the LSWR - GWR rivalry was minimal.

For the Turnchapel railmotor services, a halt was erected close to the point where

Above:- Friary shed, October 1904. 'H12' railcar No.2 took up duties on the Friary - Turnchapel branch after having been found unsuitable for its intended tasks on the Basingstoke & Alton line. It remained at Plymouth until February 1910. PHOTOGRAPH: F.H.C. CASBOURN, COURTESY R.C. RILEY

Friary station, possibly 1951/52. As we shall see later on, GWR engines - especially 2-6-0s - were regular performers on SR metals in Plymouth long before the Western Region consumed its rival. The engines seen here are 'M7' No.30036 and an unidentified '43XX'. PHOTOGRAPH: JOHN SMITH

the branch diverged from the main line to the east of Friary station. Named Lucas Terrace Halt, its platform was 120ft long and 7ft wide. The original timber platform (which seems not to have been provided with any sort of shelter at first) was eventually replaced by a platform built of the pre-cast concrete beloved of the LSWR. Most sources state that the halt came into operation in October 1905 but, on 22 May, the LSWR wrote to the Board of Trade requesting a prompt inspection *'as it is desired to bring the halt into use on 1st June'.* The report passed the halt for use on 29 June.

In Southern Railway days, Plymouth was - in theory at least - served by two named trains from Waterloo. The theoretical one of the pair was the celebrated 'Atlantic Coast Express', inaugurated on 19 July 1926. The 'ACE' was spectacularly multi-portioned and at a cursory glance the public timetables indicated that the train included a portion for Plymouth. The alleged Plymouth portion usually consisted of two coaches which left Exeter in conjunction with coaches for Bude and Padstow, the two-coach set for Plymouth being detached at Okehampton.

The caution employed in the above reference to the 'ACE' is due to the fact that the Plymouth part did not carry headboards, the boards being used only on the Ilfracombe, Torrington, Padstow and Bude carriages. It is, therefore, questionable, whether the Plymouth carriages were officially regarded as a component

of the 'ACE'. Furthermore, it is interesting to note that when a complete train (i.e. with Plymouth carriages) left Waterloo at the usual time of 11.00am, the 'ACE' designation was given instead to the 10.54am departure. A thorny subject!

The second (and indisputably) named train was the Devon Belle, an all-Pullman affair inaugurated on 20 June 1947. The 'Belle' was also multi-portioned - albeit not to the same extent as the 'ACE' - and the Plymouth portion consisted of four

Friary station, 5 May 1963. It finished its days as Plymouth's main goods depot, ceasing to handle passenger traffic from 15 September 1958, when all passenger services were subsequently concentrated at North Road. Seen here are Friary 'B' signalbox (centre foreground), which closed in July 1962, and the goods shed (extreme left), demolished in 1965/66 to make way for a new freight concentration depot. An ignominious end for what had once been an extremely pleasant - if occasionally neglected - station. PHOTOGRAPH: S.C. NASH

Left:- Passing Friary loco, 1927. In recently-applied SR livery, 'B4' 0-4-0T No.E100 heads towards Friary with the Cattewater branch goods. Because of the gradients on the branch, the little tanks were restricted to a loading of 30 wagons plus a brake.
PHOTOGRAPH: F.H.C. CASBOURN, COURTESY R.C. RILEY

Pullmans. For its first year of operation it ran each way on Fridays, Saturdays, Sundays and Mondays, but for 1948-51 a down working on Thursdays and an up on Tuesdays were added. The 'Belle' had only a brief life, the Plymouth portion being discontinued after the summer of 1949 and the entire service ceasing in September 1954.

The 'ACE' and the 'Devon Belle' obviously worked into Plymouth via Okehampton and were hauled by SR engines. Friary station and the Okehampton route were not, however, completely out

Near Friary Junction, 1927, 'B4' No.E100 approaches with a transfer goods from Laira.
PHOTOGRAPH: F.H. CASBOURN, COURTESY R.C. RILEY

of bounds to GWR engines, *The Railway Magazine* of September/October 1942 noting that: *'For some time past the GWR has been working the 7.5pm SR train from Exeter to Plymouth by the SR route, and the 2.25pm from Plymouth (Friary) to Exeter. Mogul No.7321 has been so engaged. The 4.40pm from Friary to Exeter has also been worked for some time by a GWR 2-6-0, which returns by the GWR route. By way of exchange, SR 2-6-0 No.1408 has been seen on the 11.25am stopping train from Exeter (St.Davids) to Plymouth. Pilot drivers are carried with the engine crews'.*

The above extract warrants an explanation. During the war, it was considered advisable for SR and GWR crews to fa-

miliarise themselves with each other's routes between Exeter and Plymouth in case of emergency, and those observations of 1942 signalled the start of what became known as 'exchange diagrams'. Such diagrams continued until the end of steam. A typical mid-1950s exchange diagram involved a Laira engine and crew taking the 2.25pm Friary to Exeter Central stopper and returning with the 6.35pm Exeter Central to Friary semi-fast, while an Exeter engine and crew would work the 11.47am Exeter Central to Friary stopper and the 4.40pm stopper from Friary as far as Exeter. The pilotmen referred to in the magazine extract were on board for route training purposes.

Right:- A Turnchapel branch train, hauled by 'O2' 0-4-4T No.30207, pulls away from Friary station, 7 September 1951. This picture was taken from the Tothill Road bridge, a popular (nay, obvious) vantage point for the few photographers who troubled to explore this corner of Plymouth. PHOTOGRAPH: ALAN LATHEY

Right :- Friary station, 30 August 1945. In the Plymouth area GWR locomotives routinely appeared at certain SR strongholds. When public passenger services on the Yealmpton branch were reintroduced in November 1941 - principally for the benefit of Plymothians who had moved to the countryside during the war - the services operated to and from Friary. The revival was, however, brief, services being withdrawn in October 1947, this time for good. Here, 0-6-0PT No.3705 pulls away from Friary with a Yealmpton train. PHOTOGRAPH: H.C. CASSERLEY

Left:- Oreston station, 12 January 1951. The Turnchapel branch passenger train, with 'O2' No.30182 in charge, prepares to embark on the 1 in 50 descent to Turnchapel. This train was hardly over-patronised as, apparently, the 'passenger' sheltering under the canopy was another photographer. At the time this picture was taken, 1951, the area on the east bank of the River Plym was actually outside of Plymouth, but in 1967 the city boundary was extended to incorporate Plymstock, Oreston and Turnchapel, along with other parts of the South Hams. PHOTOGRAPH: ALAN LATHEY

Turnchapel, 4 January 1951. The swing bridge carried the Turnchapel branch across the entrance to Hooe Lake. Turnchapel station was behind the photographer - i.e. on the west bank of the channel. Here, 'O2' 0-4-4T No.30182 brings the branch passenger train towards the station. Behind the trailing coach is a single-span bridge which carried the Turnchapel branch over the siding to the timber yards and creosoting works at Oreston. PHOTOGRAPH: ALAN LATHEY

Turnchapel, 19 June 1950. A two-coach gated motor set waits before commencing its return journey to Friary station. Although this was the end of the journey for passenger trains, the branch continued beyond the station (to the left on this picture) to wharves which the Admiralty had taken over in 1905, principally as a refuelling point for submarines. Behind the wharves were quarries, which also became Admiralty property and were used for oil storage.

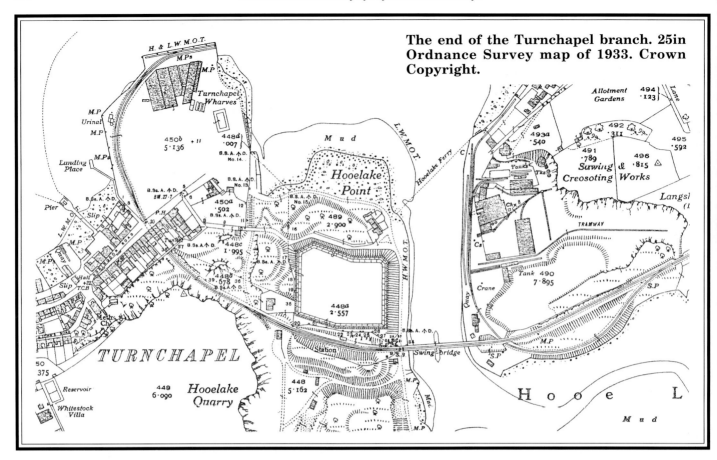

The end of the Turnchapel branch. 25in Ordnance Survey map of 1933. Crown Copyright.

Left:- Near Turnchapel, 12 January 1951. The Turnchapel branch goods, hauled by 'B4' 0-4-0T No.30094, attacks the 1 in 50 climb towards Oreston. The photographer has pointed out that the apparent protrusion from the engine's chimney is not a religious symbol, but a telegraph pole in the background. PHOTOGRAPH: ALAN LATHEY

Near Plymstock, 28 March 1951. Having collected more wagons at Plymstock, the Turnchapel branch goods heads towards Laira Bridge en route to Friary. The engine is 'B4' 0-4-0T No.30102, which is now preserved. Note the spark arrester - it was an essential requirement for engines going near the timber yards at Oreston, hence the regular appearances of such devices on Friary's B4s and occasionally O2s. PHOTOGRAPH: ALAN LATHEY

Right:- Near Friary, 5 September 1951. Drummond 'T9' No.30707 coasts towards Friary with a stopping train from Exeter. The engine had its BR number applied in May 1948 and was painted BR lined black in December 1950. It had a couple of short periods as an Exmouth Junction engine in the early 1950s. The headcode on the engine, incidentally, is that of a Class B passenger train - some crews changed the discs from the SR code at Devonport (Kings Road), but others did not. PHOTOGRAPH: ALAN LATHEY

Below right:- Devonport Tunnel South, 2 October 1952. An Exeter Central - Plymouth Friary stopping train (probably the 11.47am ex-Exeter) emerges from the tunnel on the approach to Devonport (Kings Road). The engine is Churchward Mogul No.6397, which still has its pre-Nationalisation identity emblazoned on the tender. The use of WR motive power on the SR route (and vice versa) between Plymouth and Exeter was a regular occurrence. The 'exchange' workings had been instigated in 1942 so that, in case of emergency, trains could be readily re-routed without the need for pilotmen. The practice continued until the end of steam. On the SR route, the usual pattern was for a Laira engine and crew to work the 2.25pm Friary - Exeter Central stopper and return with the 6.35pm semi-fast from Exeter Central (the Plymouth portion of the 3.0pm ex-Waterloo). An Exeter engine and crew worked the 11.47am stopping train from Exeter Central to Friary and the 4.40pm Friary - Eastleigh train (but only as far as Exeter Central). Usual engines were 43XX Moguls, but Manor 4-6-0s were regularly employed around 1948-1954 and, later, BR Standard 4MT 4-6-0s (the 75000s). As evidenced elsewhere in this book, 'Halls' also had a brief stint. PHOTOGRAPH: ALAN LATHEY

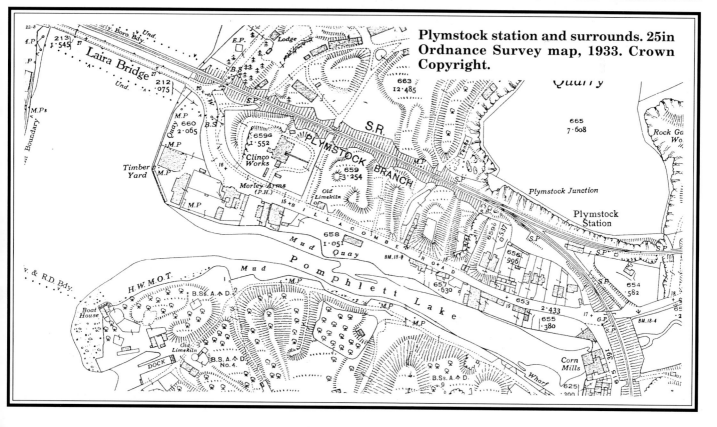

Plymstock station and surrounds. 25in Ordnance Survey map, 1933. Crown Copyright.

Laira, 10 July 1900. The roundhouse takes shape. Due to the amount of in-filling that had been necessary, the walls of the shed and the radiating roads were supported on brick arches built up from the foundations.

Chapter Three
Laira

*'As the site of the shed was formerly
a refuse pit ...'*

Laira engine shed might be regarded as the GWR's traditional home in Plymouth, but it was not built until more than half a century after the first of the company's predecessors entered Plymouth. The South Devon Railway (which was absorbed by the GWR in 1876) opened its line through to Millbay in 1849, and it had an engine shed to the north of the terminus, on the west side of the running line.

The original shed at Millbay was a 145ft long, twin-road building, constructed of stone with a slated roof, but a separate four-road shed, built mainly of timber, was added in GWR days. The precise date on which the new shed was provided seems unclear but, hazarding a guess, it could have been 1884 as, in that year, the facilities at Millbay shed were improved by the provision of a lifting shop and the replacement of the old turntable by a new 45ft example.

At the beginning of 1901, the Millbay allocation comprised 74 locomotives - twenty-eight 4-4-0s, seventeen 0-6-0s (four 'Armstrong Goods', the rest 'Dean Goods'), twenty-two assorted 0-6-0 Tanks, two 'Metro' 2-4-0Ts, one '517' class 0-4-2T, and four 0-4-0STs.

For several years, Millbay shed had been hard-pressed to cope with such a stud. Expansion was ruled out because of the cramped nature of the site, and so an alternative location was sought for a new shed. A suitable site was found at Laira, on the eastern outskirts of Plymouth, and a new shed opened there in the summer of 1901. Millbay shed was, however, retained and by the start of 1921 it still had an official allocation of thirty engines - five 4-4-0s, ten 2-6-0s, seven 2-6-2Ts (one '44XX', the others '45XXs'), six assorted 0-6-0PTs and two 0-6-0STs. Millbay was closed in July 1924, although in 1923 and again in 1924, the Locomotive Committee had put forward proposals to install electric lighting at the engine and carriage sheds at Millbay. The minutes, incidentally, referred to the premises not as Millbay, but as Harwell Street. In May 1925 - after just ten months of closure - Millbay shed was reprieved as a stabling point for ten engines because of: '....delays caused by locos getting to and from Laira through heavy track occupation'.

Millbay's reprieve lasted only until 1931, when the accommodation at Laira was enlarged. However, GWR records suggest that Millbay shed refused to dis-

appear, as the allocation lists for 1 January 1934 clearly show three 0-6-0STs and two 0-6-0PTs at 'Plymouth' (Millbay's official designation).

There was another shed at Plymouth - adjacent to a warehouse between the Inner and Outer Basins of the docks - but that was a small single-road building with no siding accommodation to speak of, and could hardly have catered for five engines.

The eventual demise of Millbay shed seems to have been a protracted affair, and the same could be said of the shed at Plymouth Docks which, despite disappearing from official registers by the mid-1940s, seems to have been used sporadically until the mid-1950s. Indeed, at the start of the BR era, on 1 January 1948, 0-6-0ST No 1365 is noted as being outstationed at 'Plymouth Docks'.

Laira shed was some two miles east of North Road station in the triangle formed by Laira Junction, Lipson Junction and Mount Gould Junction. It had been in the planning stage since at least 1896 (William Dean having requested, on 12 August of that year, authorisation for £9,000 to be spent on a new shed at Laira) and, as already mentioned, it opened around 1901. The shed was a single

'Plymouth Docks' shed, undated. This picture was taken before World War II, as the buildings in the background succumbed during the war. The practice of outstationing a Laira engine (or two) at Plymouth Docks seems to have continued until the 1950s, although the locomotive activity here is non-existent. That said, the general air of inactivity suggests that this might have been a Sunday. Whatever the case, expert photographers will be able to determine from the angle of the shadows that the time of day is a little after 1pm. The line leading off right heads towards Millbay station.

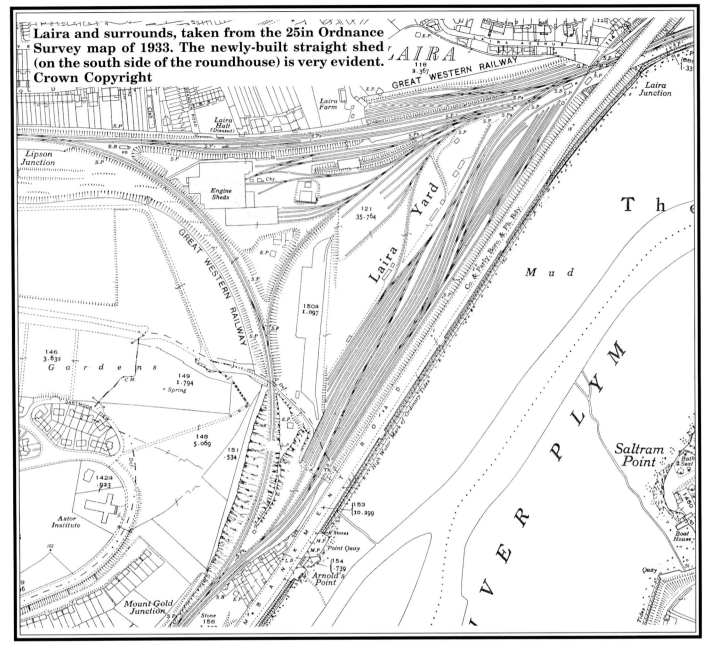

Laira and surrounds, taken from the 25in Ordnance Survey map of 1933. The newly-built straight shed (on the south side of the roundhouse) is very evident. Crown Copyright

roundhouse. In 1902 Churchward replaced Dean as Locomotive Superintendent. He had been Dean's right-hand man and, as a result of Dean's failing health had, from the late 1890s, wielded increasing power and influence. Although Dean remained in nominal charge until 1902, the fact that Churchward was awarded a substantial pay rise in 1897 confirms the latter's role.

Churchward had his own ideas about how engine sheds should be designed but, despite his probable involvement with the design of Laira shed, he soon made it clear that he was unimpressed - he wanted a completely new shed. The Locomotive Committee minutes of 20 December 1905 refer to the purchase of 20 acres or so of land at Laira *'in connection with the erection of a new Engine Shed at that place'*. The matter was further discussed on 17 July 1907: *'Referring to ... negotiations*

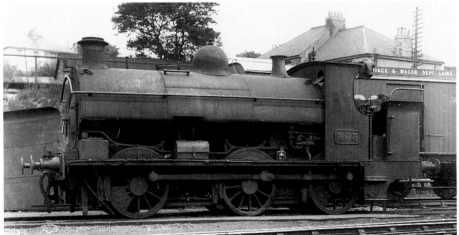

15 June 1926. '850' class 0-6-0ST No.863 was built at Wolverhampton in November 1874, was fitted with pannier tanks in October 1927, and withdrawn in May 1932. It spent all of its later life in the West Country, and was at Laira for the 'first weeks' of 1926 and 1927. It is seen on the north side of the shed yard, beneath the running lines. PHOTOGRAPH: H.C. CASSERLEY

15 June 1926. 81 'Aberdare' 2-6-0s were built between 1900 and 1907. It has often been suggested that some were rebuilds of the unsuccessful 'Kruger' 2-6-0s, but it seems that, apart from the possible re-use of some numberplates, few if any parts from 'Krugers' were actually incorporated. Although the 'Aberdares' were introduced primarily for working heavy coal trains between South Wales and Swindon, some were based at Laira, St.Blazey and Truro for working the china clay traffic. No.2620 spent many years at either Laira or St.Blazey, but was transferred out of the area in 1931, never to return; it was withdrawn from Stourbridge shed in August 1949. Note the unusual position of the 'not to be moved' board on the engine. PHOTOGRAPH H.C. CASSERLEY

being entered into for the acquisition of ... land for the site of an engine shed at Laira, the Locomotive Superintendent reported that the price asked for the land was so prohibitive that the scheme had been abandoned and that, as an alternative, he recommended the purchase of ... land adjacent to the existing engine shed at that place'.

In view of the price of land at Laira, the GWR looked at alternative sites. One scheme, reported in 1906, was for a depot in the fork between the main Exeter line and the Launceston branch at Tavistock Junction. Another proposal involved a site on the south side of the main line just to the east of Tavistock Junction. Both of those were for depots consisting of *four* roundhouses - in other words, something the size of Old Oak Common.

Churchward's liking for multi-roundhouse depots might have been considered a little over-ambitious at Plymouth. At the beginning of 1909, for example, a fairly modest total, 66 locomotives and four railmotors, was there - 47 engines and one railmotor at Millbay, and 19 engines and four railmotors at Laira. Laira's stud included a pair of 4-4-0s but, otherwise, they were almost exclusively 0-6-0 tender or tank engines. That division of engine types had, it seems, been the intention from the outset, *The Railway Magazine* of August 1901 noting that: 'The shed will be largely used for stabling goods locomotives'.

While the matter of a further shed at Laira was under protracted discussion, the facilities at Millbay were not ignored - on 8 October 1908 £625 was approved for new loco hoist. As for Laira itself 24 July 1913 there was complaint regarding: 'almost an entire absence of facilities at

Laira for unloading coal from, and loading coal into, wagons. As a consequence, when the coal stack has to be worked upon the operations have to be accomplished by wheeling - an expensive and slow method. It is therefore recommended that coal stacking sidings be installed at an esti-

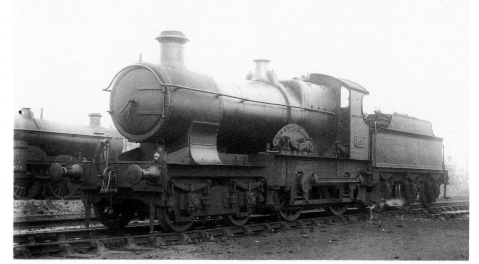

1929 - precise date unknown. The 'Bulldog' 4-4-0s augmented the earlier 'Earls' in the West Country, both classes developing a strong synonymity with the area. No.3417 was built in June 1906 as No.3707 (being renumbered in 1912), and ran nameless until February 1916 when it was christened FRANCIS MILDMAY after the newly appointed GWR Director. In July 1923 it was renamed LORD MILDMAY OF FLETE, thus reflecting Mr. M's social elevation. The engine remained in the West Country, although not as a resident of Laira shed, until 1930 when it moved to the Wolverhampton Division. It survived until the BR era, but only just, being withdrawn from Wellington shed in April 1948. PHOTOGRAPH: A.G.ELLIS

18 January 1932. An ROD 2-8-0, a 'Star', a '51XX' 2-6-2T and a '1361' 0-6-0ST can be easily identified in the roundhouse.

18 January 1932. After almost thirty years of procrastination, the facilities at Laira were finally augmented in 1932 by a new four-road straight shed, built on the south side of the existing roundhouse. ...'Steel framed with brick panels up to the underside of the steel window sashes. Between these and above them, corrugated asbestos sheeting is fixed and the roof is boarded and covered with asbestos'... let's hope that the authorities told the demolition contractors the full story in 1967.

mated cost of £654'. As for the proposed new shed, a note of May 1913 records: 'The Committee on the 2nd February 1911 authorised the acquisition of 3a 0r 39p of land at Laira - what is known as the Sewage Works site - at a cost of £2,200, to supersede the purchase of 20a 2r 28p authorised on 17th July 1907, this larger area constituting practically the whole of a Recreation Ground which is being laid down by the Plymouth Corporation.

'The Sewage Farm site has not actually been acquired for the reason that in working up the details of the plan for an engine shed it was found the foundation work would be abnormally costly owing to the great depth at which solid ground could be found.

'Further consideration has therefore had to be given to the question, and it is now proposed to revert to the Recreation Ground site, covering about 10 acres, and the Plymouth Corporation are prepared to sell this area for a sum of £9,625 provided that the Company also purchase the Sewage Farm site at the originally agreed figure of £2,200, and although the latter is not immediately required for the Company's purposes, its situation is such that it is bound in course of time to be utilised by the Company and should not be allowed in any case to fall into other hands.

'The situation at Plymouth in the matter of Locomotive accommodation has become most acute. The existing shed (at Millbay) is practically roofless, the covering having had to be removed on grounds of safety, and the staff complain of the conditions under which they have to perform their duties'.

Little more was heard of the proposals until 7 March 1914: '...owing to the necessity for considering various schemes for bettering the position, nothing has been done to the building (at Millbay) to keep it in repair. 'It has now been decided to erect a new engine shed by the side of the up line near Lipson Junction, upon land

17 December 1946. Work has started on the installation of two 82,600-gallon oil tanks in preparation for the Government's oil-burning scheme of 1947/48. But, as the history books show, the scheme was abandoned in September 1948.

7 April 1950. Churchward's '43XX' Moguls were rather more than 'middle of the road' machines - they were at home on anything from local goods to main line passenger duties, and usually performed their varied tasks with unsung efficiency. Unlike some other all-purpose classes found elsewhere in Britain, the '43XXs' had plenty of style and character. Here, No.6319, complete with red-backed number plate, stands in the yard at Laira. Note the corrugated iron coaler behind the engines, and the pre-1950 shed codes on No.6319 and the adjacent 'Grange' - LA (Laira) on the Mogul and TA (Taunton) on the Grange. PHOTOGRAPH: P.W. GRAY

purchased from the Plymouth Corporation. The new depot will be adjacent to the existing shed near Laira Junction erected on a site which does not allow of further extension.

As the accommodation is very urgently needed and the New Works Engineer is in a position to let forthwith contracts for tipping etc, I beg to recommend that the ex-penditure, estimated at £84,590, be authorised'.

Authorisation was given five days later but, after all the years of discussion, the plans were shelved as the situation deteriorated into World War I. The subject of new facilities at Laira was raised *again* in May 1923...: 'It is not anticipated that the shed will be commenced at present,

but when it is, it will be necessary to provide accommodation for an increased number of tender engines'.

In 1925 it was proposed to built a separate building on the south side of the main line just to the west of Lipson Junction. The proposal was for a quadruple-round-house depot - similar to the plans of 1906, albeit on a different site - but like the

April 1956. For many years the majority of the '3150' class 2-6-2Ts were based at Severn Tunnel Junction, but Laira usually had a small handful of representatives. No.3186 was one of Laira's regulars, and was allocated there for much of the time from 1931 until its withdrawal in June 1957. PHOTOGRAPH: RAIL ARCHIVE STEPHENSON

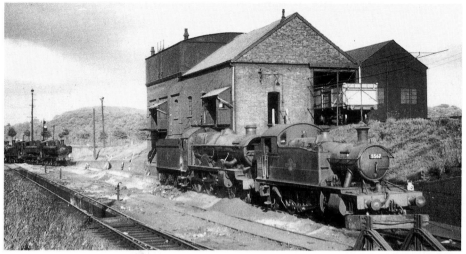

17 June 1958. The three separate components of Laira's coal stage are evident - the original stage of 1901 with water tank atop, the brick-built, slate-roofed addition of 1931, and the corrugated iron wartime structure which enabled tipping on the other side of the ramp. Seven year-old No.7031 CROMWELLS CASTLE keeps 2-6-2T No.5567 company. PHOTOGRAPH: W. POTTER

17 July 1960. The queue on the coal stage road encroaches on the through goods lines. Although this was a Sunday, it was not unknown for locos awaiting coaling to foul both goods lines on Saturdays - this was sometimes unavoidable during the peak season. PHOTOGRAPH: R.C. RILEY

fully completed until February 1932), and new signalling arrangements were provided for the modified connections with the running lines. Other aspects of the work included the extension and raising of the coal stage, and the provision of a 50-ton engine hoist to replace the old 35-ton hoist.

The 'Loans Act' improvements undertaken at Laira (and elsewhere on the GWR) were described in *The Railway Gazette* supplement of 8 December 1933:

'*Owing to the closing down of Millbay engine shed, Plymouth, the accommodation at Laira was too heavily taxed. The old shed was therefore extended, and alongside was constructed a new four-track shed 210ft long and 67ft wide, a size adopted generally as a standard for the smaller modern locomotive depots provided by the company. A store 60ft by 30ft was also built.*

'*The building is steel framed with brick panels up to the underside of the steel window sashes. Between these and above them, corrugated asbestos sheeting is fixed and the roof is boarded and covered with asbestos. Skylights cover the clerestory above each roof bay for its full length, the clerestory having side louvre ventilators. There are asbestos-sheeted smoke troughs, with uptakes at intervals, above each of the four roads, which will accommodate 12 of the largest express locomotives, and each of which is provided with an engine pit 196ft long inside the shed and a 40-ft pit beyond outside.*

'*As the site of the shed was formerly a refuse pit formed on what was originally a creek of the Laira estuary, the foundations had to be piled. One hundred and ninety-six reinforced concrete piles, 14in by 14in, were driven, varying in length from 26ft to 32ft, and on these reinforced concrete beams were moulded to form part of the walls of the engine pits. The coal stage was also extended on pile foundations and the locomotive sidings were re-modelled.*'

previous plans, that came to nothing. It took at last the 'Loans Act' of 1929 to prod the GWR into positive action. The Loan (Guarantees and Grants) Act (to give it its proper title) was a Government scheme which, by offering financial incentives for the undertaking of substantial civil engineering projects, was intended to help relieve the severe unemployment of the period. The GWR might have been a proud company, but it knew a good thing when it saw one and took extensive advantage of the Act. Among the many 'Loans Act' schemes undertaken by the GWR was the building of a four-road straight shed on the south side of the existing roundhouse at Laira.

It might not have been in the same league as the quadruple-roundhouses once envisaged by Churchward, but it was a great help. The straight shed was brought into use in 1931 (although not

12 September 1959. An example of Swindon's finest - No.6007 KING WILLIAM III - and a youthful engineman. PHOTOGRAPH: TERRY NICHOLLS

27 June 1960. One of the nice things about Laira shed - apart from the apparent 'blind eye' to non-permit visitors! - was the wide cross-section of GWR/WR motive power. In this view, for example, there is a 'County', two 'Halls', a '61XX' and, in the distance, a 'King' and what seems to be a 'Grange'. Glorious. PHOTOGRAPH: W.A.POTTER

27 June 1960. The good old days? Try telling that to the chap who is shovelling ash in what, to be honest, is only a modest breeze. PHOTOGRAPH: W.A.POTTER

After acquiring the engines formerly allocated to Millbay, Laira shed - coded LA in GWR days and 83D under BR auspices in 1950 - ran a wide variety of duties and, consequently, accommodated a cross-section of locomotive types. Laira engines travelled far and wide, one random example from *The Railway Magazine* of 1927 illustrating the 'frontier' nature of its far-flung activities: "*'Castles' from Laira (Plymouth) shed since late in July have taken turns with Newton Abbot "Stars" on the 2.22pm and 5.15pm expresses into Shrewsbury from Bristol. The engines return on the 11.30am and 12.39pm expresses the next morning. Nos.4075 CARDIFF CASTLE, 4085 BERKELEY CASTLE, 4088 DARTMOUTH CASTLE, 4095 HARLECH CASTLE, 5008 RAGLAN CASTLE, 5009 SHREWSBURY CASTLE, 5011 TINTAGEL CASTLE, and 5012 BERRY POMEROY CASTLE have been noted on these turns*".

Long-standing features of the Laira allocation lists were the short-wheelbase

'1361' 0-6-0STs, built in 1910 to replace veteran ex-Cornwall Railway engines. They were intended for dock lines, where sharp curves abounded, and all five class members had spells at Laira at one time or another. Sometimes all five were there simultaneously. Laira was also responsible for supplying engines to its sub sheds at Launceston and Princetown, the former usually having a '4500' 2-6-2T and the latter a '4400'.

Among the few regular absentees from Laira's lists were the delightful little '4800/1400' 0-4-2Ts. Panniers and Prairies were usually favoured for local passenger duties, but 0-4-2Ts Nos 4827 and 4829 nevertheless had brief spells at Laira early in 1937. The 0-4-2Ts didn't return to Laira until 1955, when their usual duties were on the Saltash - Tavistock auto trains.

After the extension of Laira shed in 1931, other relatively minor alterations took place. The sand driers were replaced in 1936, the coaling facilities were improved during the war (under an order issued by the Ministry of War Transport), and two 82,600 gallon oil tanks were installed in 1947 for the fuelling of oil-burning engines.

It has been suggested that, during the height of World War II, Laira's 'Kings' were stored overnight in a tunnel (but which one??) for protection. Whether that is true or not, one little snippet of veracity which cannot go unmentioned is that Laira was the only GWR engine shed to be immortalised on a locomotive nameplate, the engine concerned being 'Bulldog' 4-4-0 No 3326. On the subject of the 'Bulldogs', Laira still had six of the veterans at the very end of GWR days, and as the shed traditionally accommodated the cream of Swindon's crop, the presence of

11 February 1962. The Hawksworth 4,000-gallon tenders could look too austere for such stylish machines as Swindon 4-6-0s. Or was it only me who held that opinion? From front to back we have No.7022 HEREFORD CASTLE, No.1006 COUNTY OF CORNWALL and No.1003 COUNTY OF WILTS. For the record, No.1006 was a Laira engine at the time and was paired with tender No.110, while No.1003 was at Shrewsbury with tender No.128. PHOTOGRAPH: TERRY NICHOLLS

22 April 1962. And another splendid line up at Laira - '45XX', 'Hall', 'Hall', 'Hall', 'Castle', 'Castle', 'County'. PHOTOGRAPH: TERRY NICHOLLS

22 April 1962. The straight shed of 1932 is well filled. Two roads of the straight shed had been screened off in 1957 for use by diesels and it was largely given over to the new traction as numbers increased. In the brief period between the new diesel depot becoming available and the final expulsion of steam, the 'straight' or 'long' shed reverted for a short time to steam. PHOTOGRAPH: TERRY NICHOLLS

57XX, 13XX, 54XX, 64XX, small tanks.
Turntables: 1 x 65ft diameter
Number of berth roads per turntable: 28
Area of shed: 434ft x 181ft - 78,554sqft
Perimeter of shed: 1230ft 0in
Height to eaves: 21ft 0in
Height to ridge: 26ft 9in
Inside headroom: 16ft 0in, but 13ft 10in at door
Materials of construction: Walls - brick; roof - steel trusses and asbestos sheeting part glazed; floor - brickwork
Area of windows: 305sqft
Percentage of Window area to Wall area: 1.9%
Percentage of projected top Glazing to Floor area: 13.9%
Artificial lighting: Shed - electric; pits - nil; portable - electric hand lamps, flare lamps, acetylene lamps
Pits: 28 inspection pits (4 x 41ft, 8 x 43ft, 8 x 48ft, 8 x 60ft)
Wheel drops: nil
Cranes: Hoist in Lifting Shop; 35ton Engine Hoist (?); 20ton Engine Hoist; 2ton Coaling Crane
Compressed air points: 9
Steam (boiler washing) points: 14
Smoke chutes: 28 (25 x 11ft, 1 x 61ft, 1 x 61ft 9in, 1 x 56ft - all 3ft 3in wide)
Accommodation: Stores - 1710sqft; office - 724sqft; canteen - one 64ft dining car and one kitchen car, seating capacity 64
Washing facilities: 3 washing troughs and 5 wash basins
Area of Yard: 375,000sqft
Number of access roads: 3
Minimum curve: 6° chain radius
Maximum gradient, excluding coal stage: 1 in 125
Number of sidings: 3
Length of sidings: 890ft
Number of roads per throat track: 8

outside-framed 4-4-0s as late as 1947 might seem surprising. The explanation is that they were required for piloting 'Kings' on the South Devon banks, the working instructions stating that any engine used in front of a 'King' must have four or more driving wheels and a bogie.

FOOTNOTE 1
In March 1947 the GWR conducted a survey of major engine sheds which had been built within the previous 25-30 years, and Laira was among those scrutinised. Perversely, the official report concentrated on the 46 year-old roundhouse and completely ignored the 1931 straight shed (not exactly in keeping with the brief!), but it included fairly comprehensive details of the structure and its facilities:
Number of engines allocated: 101
Classes allocated: 60XX, 50XX, 10XX, 49XX, 33XX, 48XX, 47XX, 28XX, Austerity, 43XX, 31XX, 51XX, 45XX, 44XX,

30 April 1961. No.6400 undergoing repairs. Laira had two hoists, one of 35 tons and the other of 20 tons. PHOTOGRAPH: R.C. RILEY

Number of switches: 25
Number of Catch Points: One
Length of plain line: 4875ft; sidings 890ft; coal stage 410ft; Total 6175ft
Coaling arrangements: Gradient 1 in 30; total length 410ft; capacity 5 x 20ton wagons (full); two locos served simultaneously, coal dumps of 10,000tons capacity
Ash pits: 2 (1 x 242ft long; 1 x 120ft long)
Ash handling: 2ton crane with grab; also by hand
Examination pits: 1 at 225ft; 4 at 60ft; 1 at 65ft
Number of water columns: 5

FOOTNOTE 2
Laira allocation list - 1 January 1948
'County' 4-6-0: 1004 COUNTY OF SOMERSET, 1006 COUNTY OF CORNWALL, 1009 COUNTY OF CARMARTHEN
'Castle' 4-6-0: 4032 QUEEN ALEXANDRA, 4087 CARDIGAN CASTLE, 4088 DARTMOUTH CASTLE, 4090 DORCHESTER CASTLE, 5009 SHREWSBURY CASTLE, 5026 CRICCIETH CASTLE, 5041 TIVERTON CASTLE, 5050 EARL OF ST.GERMANS, 5057 EARL WALDEGRAVE, 5060 EARL OF BERKELEY, 5090 NEATH ABBEY, 5095 BARBURY CASTLE
'Hall' 4-6-0: 4966 SHAKENHURST HALL, 5998 TREVOR HALL, 6907 DAVENHAM HALL, 6913 LEVENS HALL
Oil-burning 'Hall' 4-6-0: 3901(4971) STANWAY HALL, 3902(4948) NORTHWICK HALL, 3955(6949) HABERFIELD HALL
'King' 4-6-0: 6000 KING GEORGE V, 6002 KING WILLIAM IV, 6004 KING GEORGE III, 6010 KING CHARLES I, 6012 KING EDWARD VI, 6016 KING EDWARD V, 6017 KING EDWARD IV, 6019 KING HENRY V, 6020 KING HENRY IV, 6022 KING EDWARD III, 6026 KING JOHN, 6029 KING EDWARD VIII
'Bulldog' 4-4-0: 3391 DOMINION OF CANADA, 3401 VANCOUVER, 3431, 3441 BLACKBIRD, 3445 FLAMINGO, 3446 GOLDFINCH

Above:- 11 March 1962. The first series of '45XX' class 2-6-2Ts, Nos.4500-4574, had straight-top 1,000-gallon tanks, the later engines having sloping-top 1,300-gallon tanks. The first series therefore had lower axle weights - 14tons 10cwt instead of 15tons 11cwt - and, consequently, were permitted on some branches where their heavier brethren were prohibited. Here, No.4567 is under the hoist while No.4574 awaits completion of its own repairs. PHOTOGRAPH: TERRY NICHOLLS

Below:- 11 February 1962. The 'Granges' were, perhaps, similar to the '43XX' Moguls in that, despite being highly useful engines, they were often ignored by many enthusiasts. A shame - they deserved wider recognition. No.6825 LLANVAIR GRANGE, seemingly displaying a Penzance shedplate, enjoys the winter sunshine. PHOTOGRAPH: TERRY NICHOLLS

'2800' 2-8-0: 2857, 2867, 3811, 3864
Oil-burning '2800' 2-8-0: 4807 (2848), 4808 (2834), 4811 (2847), 4855 (3813)
'4700' 2-8-0: 4703
'4300' 2-6-0: 5318, 5376, 6319
'3150' 2-6-2T: 3186, 3187
'4500' 2-6-2T: 4517, 4528, 4531, 4542, 4583, 4591 ,5540, 5567, 5569
'5100' 2-6-2T: 5148
'1701' 0-6-0PT: 1799

15 April 1962. No.4918 DARTINGTON HALL, a resident of Cardiff Canton near the Laira coalstage. A 45XX 2-6-2T is on coal stage duties - this was normally the preserve of 0-6-0PTs. PHOTOGRAPH: TERRY NICHOLLS

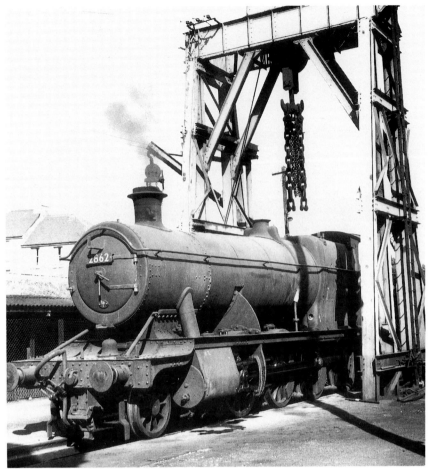

11 February 1962. Severn Tunnel Junction's '28XX' No.2862 simmers at Laira. It seems to be nothing more than a coincidence that the engine is parked under the hoist, as the official registers make no mention of it undergoing any repairs at Laira at that time. An 'unclassified' was, however, required at Ebbw Junction shops in April 1962. The '28XXs', which were sometimes used on passenger trains at peak times, worked right through to Penzance, whereas their larger colleagues, the '47XXs' ('Long Toms'), were, like the 'Kings', prohibited from crossing not only the Royal Albert Bridge, but also Keyham Viaduct. That said, 'Kings' are known to have ventured across the Tamar into Cornwall in 1938 and on another occasion in the late 1950s. PHOTOGRAPH: TERRY NICHOLLS

'1901' 0-6-0PT: 1973, 1990
'2700' 0-6-0PT: 2776
'5700' 0-6-0PT: 3629, 3639, 3675, 3686, 3705, 3787, 3790, 4653, 4656, 4658, 4679, 4693, 7762, 8709, 8719, 9711, 9716, 9765, 9770
'5400' 0-6-0PT: 5412
'6400' 0-6-0PT: 6406, 6414, 6417, 6419, 6421
'1361' 0-6-0ST: 1361, 1363, 1364 1365 *
WD 2-8-0: 77161(90148), 77196(90173), 77255(90212), 77294(90359), 77325 (90237), 77421(90292), 78671(90642), 78717(90658)
* No 1365 was outstationed at Plymouth Docks shed.
Not shown - '4400' 2-6-2Ts Nos 4402 and 4407 at Princetown and '4500' 2-6-2T No

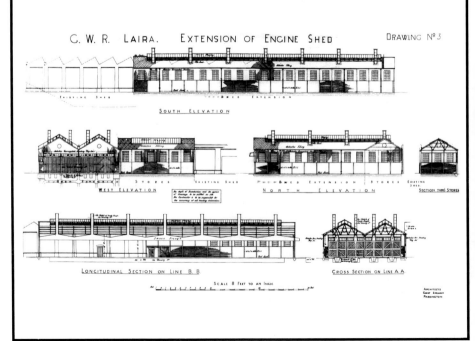

Laira Junction, 6 August 1959. The 12.05 Plymouth to Paddington is hauled by No.6004 KING GEORGE III with No.6833 CALCOT GRANGE piloting. During the winter, when train loadings were often lighter, up expresses did not always require assistance from Plymouth, and this often left Laira's 'Manors' at something of a loose end until the piloting season returned. The boarded crossing in the foreground is that of the 4ft 6in gauge horse-worked Lee Moor Tramway. Auto coaches W166W and W225W stand in the sidings on the right and the single carriage to the left of the signalbox is W2345W. Disconcertingly for traditionalists, the mobile cranes in the left distance are engaged on preparatory work for the new diesel depot. PHOTOGRAPH: P.W. GRAY

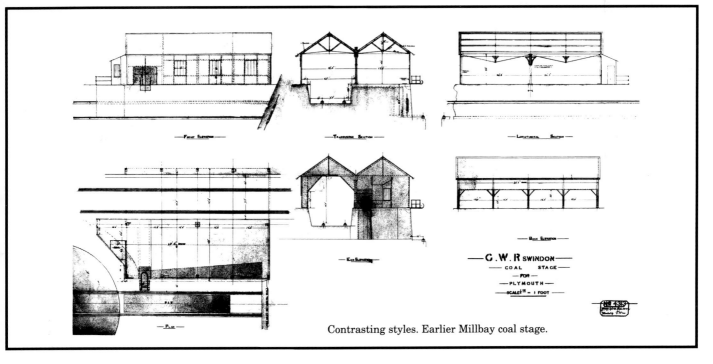

Contrasting styles. Earlier Millbay coal stage.

The first engine shed at Friary was almost alongside the station. It is clearly marked on this 25in Ordnance Survey map of 1914. Crown Copyright.

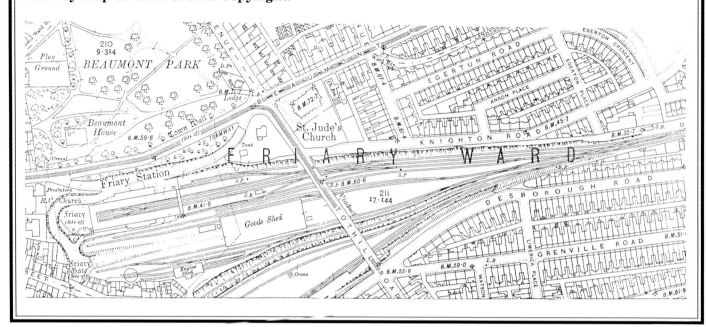

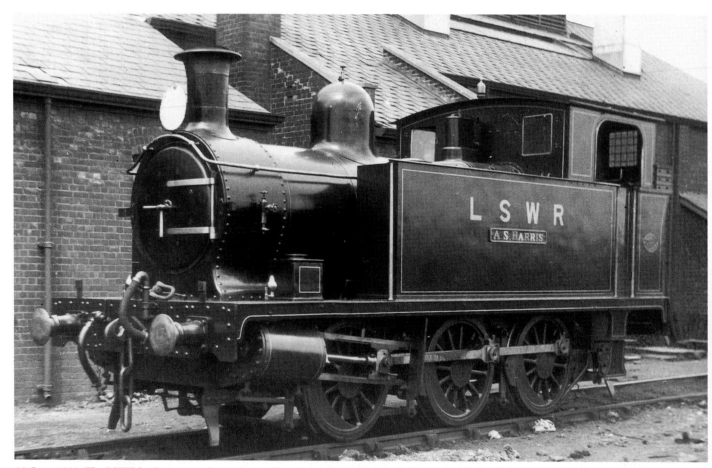

30 June 1923. The LSWR had on several occasions offered to work the Plymouth Devonport & South Western Junction Railway's Callington branch until eventually the larger company actually absorbed the PD&SWJR. Permission for the absorption was granted on 11 December 1922 (only three weeks before, and as a prelude to, the grouping) but, as if to make the most of its last three weeks of independence, the LSWR promptly applied its initials to the three PD&SWJR locomotives. The three were an 0-6-0T named A.S.HARRIS and two 0-6-2Ts, EARL OF MOUNT EDGCUMBE and LORD ST.LEVAN, and these were allotted LSWR Nos.756, 757 and 758 respectively. Prior to the grouping they had been repaired at Callington, the last to be overhauled there being A.S.HARRIS which returned to traffic - in a form of LSWR livery, albeit without its new number - in June 1923. It is seen alongside Friary shed, presumably fresh from its Callington overhaul. PHOTOGRAPH: F.H.C. CASBOURN, COURTESY R.C. RILEY

Chapter Four

Friary

'...A perfect death trap...'

Friary was not the first LSWR engine shed in the Plymouth area - a small establishment had been provided behind the north-west platform at Devonport when that station opened in May 1876. It had two roads, which converged to meet just short of a 40ft turntable; each could accommodate little more than a single tender engine, and it seems that the only additional stabling space available was in the goods yard.

Among the engines accommodated at Devonport from the start were, almost certainly, some of the six 4-4-0Ts (Nos 318-323) built for the LSWR by Beyer Peacock in 1876 to the same basic design as the celebrated Metropolitan Railway 4-4-0Ts. The LSWR engines proved to be very rough riders, and were quickly replaced by older tried-and-tested steeds, including Adams 4-4-2Ts. The new Adams '395' class 0-6-0s (introduced in 1881) soon found employment on secondary passenger and goods workings between Plymouth and Exeter, and Adams distinctive 'Jubilee' 0-4-2s (constructed between 1887 and 1895) also worked the line early on. By the late 1880s the LSWR was plan-

ning the conversion of its goods station at Friary into a passenger terminus, and preliminary moves were being made to provide a new engine shed at Friary. Although little was heard of the proposal until 1890, a Locomotive Committee minute of November 1888 seemed to anticipate savings: '...*letter received from the Locomotive Superintendent as to the arrangements of the Driver's and Firemen's duties at Devonport, by which there will be a saving of about 29s/6d per week in overtime and the allowance of £10 per annum hitherto paid to the Station Master at Devonport for keeping the Locomotive Department returns will cease*'.

The new shed at Friary opened late in 1890. It was on the south side of the station but although it had the luxury of a 50ft turntable, the building itself was no larger than the one at Devonport. Both roads ran through the shed (one to the turntable), and so there was at least a little extra space for stabling. Friary shed was accordingly soon outgrown, but there was no scope for expansion at the site. In November 1904 Dugald Drummond reported that, housing only two tender and

two tank engines, it was 'inadequate for present requirements' and he recommended a 'new shed be erected to stable 15 Engines on ground belonging to the Company outside the Station'. The ground in question was to the south side of the running lines between Bulmer Road and the (then unbuilt) Lucas Terrace Halt.

It seems that little urgency was attached to the construction of the new shed, and approval (see *LSWR Engine Sheds* Irwell Press, 1990) was not given until November 1905; the plans were not sanctioned until April 1906, and the building was not finished until 1908. The new Friary shed, which cost £19,500, had three roads running through the shed to converge on the approach to the 50ft turntable. The coaling road was also connected to the 'table.

It is believed that the original shed at Friary station then closed. The older shed at Devonport, however, certainly remained open, principally to house the engines engaged on shunting duties at Stonehouse Pool and Devonport Goods. The removal of the Devonport turntable was authorised in May 1917 - '*original*

23 February 1924. The lifting road at Friary was alongside the south wall of the shed. Here, PD&SWJR 0-6-2T LORD ST.LEVAN (later SR No.758) is receiving attention. The engine survived until December 1956 (as BR No. 30758), its companion, EARL OF MOUNT EDGCUMBE, lasting until the end of 1957 (as BR No.30757); both had been transferred to Eastleigh in mid-1956 to see out their days.
PHOTOGRAPH: F.H.C. CASBOURN, COURTESY R.C. RILEY

16 July 1924. The Friary turntable is not best remembered for its qualities of balance and, in order to make things just that little bit easier, tender engines were usually turned before they had taken on water. The engine here is non-superheated 'T9' 4-4-0 No.712, complete with splasher sandboxes (which it later lost) and the customary Drummond 'watercart'. It became BR No.30712 in July 1949, was reliveried in BR lined black in April 1952, and was withdrawn in November 1958. PHOTOGRAPH: H.C. CASSERLEY

cost £520, estimated cost of removal £80, estimated value £54, estimated savings for maintenance £6.10s.0d' - and it appears that the shed itself finally fell into disuse around 1919. The building was subsequently used for private commercial purposes, and was still there when the station closed to passengers in 1964.

As the size of main line locomotives increased, the facilities at Friary had to be updated. A new lifting crane was installed in the late 1920s, and in 1938 it was recommended that the floor of the coal stage be raised by 18 inches, at an estimated cost of £300 '...in order to minimise difficulties and delay at present experienced in coaling the high tenders fitted to modern engines'.

Apart from the new crane and the alterations to the coal stage, the only real changes were the erection of a set of shear-legs (from Callington) in 1908, a new ashpit alongside the coal stage in 1920, corrugated sheeting to replace the glazing which had been badly damaged during World War Two, and re-roofing in the 1950s.

Among the engines dealt with at Friary early on were Adams '460' class 4-4-0s. In 1884 Exeter shed received brand-new Nos 147 and 460, 461 and 462, and although it is not possible to confirm how much use was made of the engines on the Plymouth road, it is known that Nos 463 and 478 were transferred to Exeter in June 1890 primarily to help out on the new route into Devonport via the

PDSWJR. The '460s' had 6ft 7in driving wheels - perhaps not ideal for the nature of the new PDSWJR line - but nine of the '380' class 4-4-0s (the 'Steamrollers', which had 5ft 7in coupled wheels) were also transferred to Exeter and Plymouth in June 1890, principally for slow passenger and pick-up goods workings.

It is known that 'T3' 4-4-0s also worked the Plymouth - Exeter route from the late 1890s but it seems none was ever actually shedded at Friary. As related in the

British Railways Illustrated Annual No 2 (Irwell Press 1993), the 'T3s' failed to impress the irascible Ernest Ahrons, who noted that one member of the class '...at one time had a dubious reputation in the matter of steam, and would saunter down the line pending developments on the part of its boiler in the direction of producing that somewhat necessary motive fluid'.

For the through services on the Plymouth - Okehampton - Exeter route, 4-4-0s (including Drummond's legendary

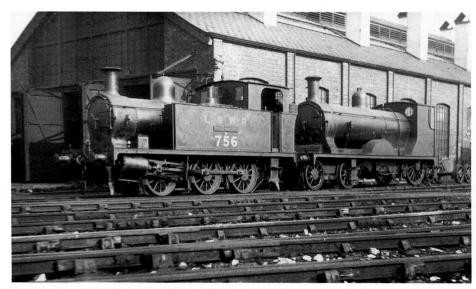

26 December 1924. Ex-PD&SWJR 0-6-0T A.S.HARRIS was inscribed with its SR number in March 1924. Behind it on the lifting road at Friary is an 'L11' 4-4-0 complete with smokebox wingplates. PHOTOGRAPH: F.H.C. CASBOURN, COURTESY R.C. RILEY

8 March 1924. The lifting road at Friary certainly seemed to attract photographic attention. This time, the engine is LORD ST.LEVAN, one of the ex-PD&SWJR Hawthorn Leslie 0-6-2Ts. PHOTOGRAPH: F.H.C. CASBOURN, COURTESY R.C. RILEY

1 April 1925. There were 'B4' 0-4-0Ts at Friary until 1959, used on the Turnchapel, Stonehouse Pool, Sutton Harbour and Cattewater branches, as well as transfer trips to and from Laira Sidings. No.100 was one of several sold into industrial use in 1949. The Adams chimneys were less than a triumph, aesthetically... PHOTOGRAPH: F.H.C. CASBOURN, COURTESY R.C. RILEY

ber yards which, in later years at least, supplied sleepers to the GWR. For Oreston duties, the engines were fitted with spark arresters. One of Friary's long-standing resident 'B4s', No 84, was the last locomotive to be built at Nine Elms Works (in 1908) before the LSWR moved its Locomotive Department to Eastleigh.

At the grouping, the SR inherited the Plymouth, Devonport & South Western Junction Railway which, in 1908, had reopened the Bere Alston - Callington branch as a standard gauge passenger-carrying line. The three PDSWJR engines (two 0-6-2Ts and one 0-6-0T) became SR stock and were nominally allocated to Friary, which was the parent of the small shed at Callington. The 0-6-0T - No 756 A.S. HARRIS - was transferred away in 1929, but the 0-6-2Ts - No 757 EARL OF MOUNT EDGCUMBE and No 758 LORD ST.LEVAN - remained in the Plymouth area until the early 1950s, and were often used on Friary's general shunting duties and the Callington branch goods.

In January 1933, the Friary allocation was 27 engines:
'B4' 0-4-0T: 84, 92, 99, 100
'O2' 0-4-4T: 182, 185, 194, 203, 212, 225, 231
'T1' 0-4-4T: 9, 71, 361, 363, 364
'T9' 4-4-0: 116, 280, 289, 709, 714, 715, 718, 722, 733
PDSW 0-6-2T: 757, 758

On the motive power front, the most conspicuous post-war change in Plymouth was, arguably, the debut of Bulleid's controversial but highly versatile lightweight Pacifics. It had been intended that the first twenty should be allocated to Exmouth Junction, but two were sent elsewhere for trials, albeit temporarily. Class members made their debut on the Exeter - Plymouth route in October 1945 - five months after the first of the class had entered traffic - but Friary didn't re-

'Greyhounds') retained a virtual monopoly until the mid-1920s, when 'N' class 2-6-0s started to appear. The 'Ns' were followed, in 1936/37, by 'U1' 2-6-0s, but neither type was allocated to Friary shed with any real regularity. Local workings - mainly to Tavistock and Okehampton but also, after the demise of the railmotors, on the Turnchapel branch - were, from the late 1890s, the domain of Adams 'T1' and 'O2' 0-4-4Ts. Drummond's 'M7' 0-4-4Ts did not gravitate westwards in numbers for some time, and even by 1937 only one (No 35) was shown on the Friary complement, its usual duties being Tavistock and Brentor locals.

The distinctive little 'B4' 0-4-0Ts were a regular feature at Friary from as early as the 1890s. Their duties included the Stonehouse Pool, Cattewater and Turnchapel lines, transfer trips to and from Laira, and shunting at Oreston tim-

8 November 1924. 'O2' No.233 had received its SR livery and 'E' prefix less than a month before this picture was taken. Around half-a-dozen of the class were usually based at Friary, used on the St.Budeaux and Tavistock locals, the Turnchapel motor trains, the Stonehouse Pool and Keyham goods, and for piloting at Devonport and Friary. PHOTOGRAPH: F.H.C. CASBOURN, COURTESY R.C. RILEY

ceive an allocation until April 1948. The initial complement was five - later, it was rare for Friary to have more than four Pacifics simultaneously - 34003 PLYMOUTH, 34011 TAVISTOCK, 34012 LAUNCESTON, 34013 OKEHAMPTON and 34021 DARTMOOR, named after places nearest to Plymouth. Initially, they worked no farther afield than Exeter, albeit mainly with Waterloo trains, but in February 1950 the Southern Region extended many of its engine workings and, from then on, the Friary Pacifics were given the job of hauling the Plymouth - Brighton through trains as far as Salisbury and, of course, the return leg from Salisbury to Plymouth. A snippet of total irrelevance - the Plymouth - Brighton trains passed through *both* SR Ford stations, the one at Plymouth and the one east of Chichester.

Throughout most of the early- and mid-1950s, Friary's usual allocation of Pacifics comprised 34035 SHAFTESBURY, 34036 WESTWARD HO, 34037 CLOVELLY and

30 August 1945. Like many parts of Plymouth, Friary shed did not escape damage during the war. Indeed, the coal stage building was totally destroyed and four men killed during the awful raids of March 1941. Here, the wartime damage to the glazed panels at the end of the shed is clearly evident. The engine wearing the spark arrester is 'B4' No.91.
PHOTOGRAPH: H.C. CASSERLEY

23 June 1949. The highly versatile Bulleid Pacifics might have revolutionised the face of motive power on many SR routes, but they weren't without their problems. One of the less publicised grumbles was that they were too long to fit on the turntable at Friary shed, and so they turned instead on the Cattewater or Lipson triangles - that said, the poorly balanced manual 'table at Friary wouldn't have been particularly useful for a Pacific. On Sundays and Bank Holidays turning was done on the Lipson triangle, as the Cattewater Junction signalbox was closed. Here, recently renumbered No.34001 EXETER passes the site of Lucas Terrace halt while using the Cattewater triangle, after working from Exeter via Newton Abbot - a routine 'exchange' working intended to familiarise WR and SR crews with each other's routes. PHOTOGRAPH: S.C. NASH

34038 LYNTON. All four were, however, transferred to Exmouth Junction in October 1957, and their diagrams went with them. The 'air-smoothed' Pacifics (Bulleid positively loathed the word 'streamlined') presented a problem at Friary, as they could not be turned at the shed - instead, they were turned on the Cattewater or

Lipson triangles. On their usual Plymouth - Exeter workings, the loadings of the trains were normally well within the Pacifics' grasp. Outside of peak times, it was far from uncommon to see a Pacific at the head of no more than three coaches.

Engine sheds - like many other places of manual work - had their fair share of

industrial accidents. Accidents on the railways were routinely investigated by the Board of Trade, and one such inquiry looked into an accident involving one George A.Glass at Friary sidings on 12 September 1929. The reporting officer, J.P.S. Main, explained that: '*Glass, who is a little over 16 years of age, is employed*

10 August 1951. Drummond 'T9' No.30717 passes Friary shed. (on the extreme left) with the 2.25pm Friary - Waterloo train. Much of the shed yard could be seen from a passing train but, frustratingly, most of the resident engines were partly (or wholly) hidden from view. Still, the walk from Friary station back to the shed - via Knighton Road, Bulmer Road and Desborough Road - wasn't too time consuming. The platform on the left is Lucas Terrace Halt, which closed exactly one month after this picture was taken. The 'M7' alongside the shed on the left is on the run-round road which was added during World War II; the new road was referred to as the 'Income Tax Road' - a reference to how, according to the staff, it had been paid for. PHOTOGRAPH: ALAN LATHEY

as a greaser lad. He had been on duty 1 hour and 25 minutes when the occurrence took place. At 7.25am, while he was attending to a goods train with which certain shunting movements were being made, the train was drawn up along the shunting neck to make a further shunt. At the moment Glass was at the side of the wagons and between them and what is described as the mileage bank, which is formed of rough shale rock. The clearance between the bank, which is a little over 3 feet in height, and the outer rail of the shunting neck varies from 3 feet 6 inches to 4 feet. While Glass was walking at the

17 June 1958. After the war, corrugated sheeting was used to repair the damaged Friary gables, and the building was re-roofed in the 1950s. The shed was transferred to the Western Region in February 1958, as evidenced by the 83H shed-plates of 'M7' 0-4-4T No.30035. Fellow No.30034 is in the background. PHOTOGRAPH: W. POTTER

5 May 1963. The Bulleid Pacifics were a regular feature at Friary, but until 1959 the rebuilt versions were prohibited from the Exeter - Plymouth line. Here, a well turned-out Exmouth Junction example, 34036 WESTWARD HO, percolates during the very last month of the shed's operational life. PHOTOGRAPH: S.C. NASH

side of the wagons in the direction of movement some part of his clothing was caught, it is assumed, by the end of a wagon brake shaft and he was drawn down and dragged along, his left leg being subsequently run over.

'Glass was perfectly aware of the movement that was being made. It never occurred to him that there was a possibility that owing to the lack of clearance he might be caught by some portion of one of the wagons. The accident may be attributed to misadventure, but in connection therewith the necessity for increasing the clearance as between the mileage bank and the shunting neck and siding is highly desirable, not only in connection with ex-

amination work, but also for the safety of the staff engaged in shunting operations. At present, owing to this lack of clearance, the whole of the work in connection with shunting movements has to be undertaken from the other side adjacent to the down main line, which is only 6 feet distant therefrom. The men have, I understand, often to pass over on to the down main line for signalling purposes owing to the curvature of the lines. If sufficient clearance were provided on the inside of the curve, which is the favourable side, the men could work in comparative freedom and away from the adjacent running line. 'The place is described to me by the men who work there as being "A perfect death

trap" and action on the part of the Company to improve conditions as suggested appears to be demanded. Further, the examination and greasing of trains during shunting operations should be avoided as far as possible, and it is suggested that arrangements should be made to accomplish this work while the trains are at a standstill before shunting operations commence'.

After Nationalisation at the end of 1947, Friary shed assumed the code 72D. The allocation lists for August 1950 featured 23 engines - the following list uses the allotted BR numbers, but it should be noted that some still wore their old SR numbers at the time. Indeed, when the 'T1' was withdrawn in May 1951 it still carried SR No 7.

'T1' 0-4-4T: 30007
'M7' 0-4-4T: 30035, 30037, 30107, 30356, 30375,
'B4' 0-4-0T: 30084, 30088, 30094, 30102 GRANVILLE
'O2' 0-4-4T: 30182, 30183, 30207, 30216, 30236
PDSW 0-6-2T: 30757, 30758
'N' 2-6-0: 31871
'E1R' 0-6-2T: 32094
'WC' 4-6-2: 34011 TAVISTOCK, 34012 LAUNCESTON, 34013 OKEHAMPTON, 34021 DARTMOOR

15 July 1958. Ivatt 2-6-2Ts made their debut on the Callington branch in September 1952, and four of the class were usually allocated to Friary until the shed's closure. PHOTOGRAPH R.C.RILEY

TRAIN WORKING : PLYMOUTH (FRIARY) : MAY 1932

Train	Arr	Dep	Destination
18.00 WATERLOO	**00.05**		
		00.50	Exmouth Jcn (News)
		01.58	*Exmouth Jcn (Goods)*
15.35 Templecombe (Goods)	*04.44*		
		05.20	*Light to Devonport*
		05.35	Turnchapel
		05.52	Salisbury
05.55 Turnchapel	06.05		
		06.11	St Budeaux
		06.15	*Exmouth Jcn (Goods)*
		06.20	Turnchapel
01.30 WATERLOO	**06.31**		
21.35 Nine Elms (Goods)	*06.40*		
06.33 Turnchapel	06.43		
		06.35	Light to Laira
		06.48	Turnchapel
06.05 Tavistock	06.53		
06.55 Laira (Goods)	*07.01*		
		07.10	Exeter
07.03 Turnchapel	07.13		
		07.18	Turnchapel
		07.22	*Cattewater (Goods)*
		07.38	Tavistock
07.32 Turnchapel	07.42		
		07.50	Turnchapel
		08.07	St Budeaux
		08.12	*Exmouth Jcn (Goods)*
08.02 Turnchapel	08.12		
		08.16	Turnchapel
01.50 Templecombe (Goods)	*08.20*		
		08.25	**WATERLOO**
08.30 Turnchapel	08.40		
07.55 Bere Alston	08.42		
		08.48	Turnchapel
07.58 Tavistock	08.54		
		09.00	*Sutton Harbour (Goods)*
09.03 Turnchapel	09.13		
09.15 Sutton Harbour (Goods)	*09.20*		
08.55 St Budeaux	09.21		
		09.30	Bere Alston
		09.40	Turnchapel
09.57 Turnchapel	10.07		
		10.10	**WATERLOO**
07.30 Exeter	10.10		
		10.30	Exeter
		10.40	Turnchapel
		10.50	*Laira (Goods)*
07.05 Okehampton (Goods)	*11.01*		
		11.05	**WATERLOO**
11.03 Turnchapel	11.13		
08.46 Exeter	11.18		
11.30 Laira (Goods)	*11.26*		
		11.27	Turnchapel
11.42 Turnchapel	11.52		
		12.10	St Budeaux
		12.15	Turnchapel
11.49 Bere Alston	12.30		
12.28 Turnchapel	12.38		
		12.48	Turnchapel
		12.57	St Budeaux
13.03 Turnchapel	13.13		

TRAIN WORKING : PLYMOUTH (FRIARY) : MAY 1932

Train	Arr	Dep	Destination
		13.19	Tavistock
		13.25	Turnchapel
13.02 St Budeaux	13.27		
13.39 Turnchapel	13.49		
13.47 Chacewater (goods)	*13.53*		
13.39 St Budeaux	14.04		
		14.05	Turnchapel
		14.08	*Plymstock (Goods)*
		14.10	**WATERLOO**
14.20 Turnchapel	14.30		
		14.35	Exeter
07.58 Salisbury	14.43		
		14.45	*Chacewater (Goods)*
		14.58	*Laira (Goods)*
		15.10	St Budeaux
08.40 WATERLOO	**15.12**		
		15.16	Turnchapel
15.30 Turnchapel	15.40		
15.55 Laira (Goods)	*15.42*		
		15.50	**WATERLOO**
		16.05	Tavistock
		16.18	Turnchapel
		16.31	St Budeaux
11.00 WATERLOO	**16.33**		
16.14 Bayleys Sdg (Goods)	*16.36*		
		16.40	Exeter
16.33 Turnchapel	16.43		
16.22 St Budeaux	16.47		
		16.57	Turnchapel
		17.10	Tavistock
16.22 Tavistock	17.15		
		17.18	*Nine Elms (Goods)*
17.09 Turnchapel	17.19		
		17.25	Turnchapel
17.10 St Budeaux	17.35		
		17.39	Turnchapel
17.10 Bere Alston	17.42		
17.39 Turnchapel	17.51		
		18.01	Turnchapel
15.21 Exeter	18.12		
		18.15	*Sutton Harbour (goods)*
		18.17	Tavistock
18.14 Turnchapel	18.24		
18.30 Sutton Harbour (Goods)	*18.35*		
		18.36	Turnchapel
18.26 Turnchapel	18.36		
12.40 WATERLOO	**18.52**		
08.55 Yeoford (Goods)	*19.08*		
		19.09	Exeter
19.07 Turnchapel	19.17		
		19.30	Turnchapel
		19.40	*Laira (Goods)*
18.50 Tavistock	19.46		
		20.07	*Yeoford (Goods)*
20.05 Turnchapel	20.15		
		20.20	Turnchapel
20.18 Laira (Goods)	*20.25*		
15.00 WATERLOO	**20.40**		
20.36 Cattewater (Goods)	*20.42*		
20.40 Turnchapel	20.50		
20.15 Tavistock	21.06		
		21.09	Turnchapel
		21.15	Tavistock
21.22 Turnchapel	21.32		
		21.55	Turnchapel
		22.15	*Yeovil Jcn (Goods)*
22.15 Turnchapel	22.25		
22.22 Laira (Goods)	*22.28*		
		22.31	Turnchapel
20.07 Exeter	22.36		
22.43 Turnchapel	22.53		
		23.00	Turnchapel
22.25 light ex Tavistock	*23.16*		
23.26 light ex Devonport	*23.41*		

The 'E1R' 0-6-2T in the above list was one of the ten ex-LB&SCR 'E1' 0-6-0Ts which had been converted in 1927-29, principally for duties on the Torrington - Halwill line in North Devon. In mid-1941 Nos 2608 and 2610 spent a few months at Friary, but the first long-term allocation there was of No 32094, which arrived in October 1949. It was used mainly in Friary goods yard, where some of the duties were beyond the scope of 'O2s' or 'B4s'.

During the 1950s Friary shed became something of a backwater, and its transfer to the Western Region in 1958 did little for its long-term future. More of this anon...

Plymouth Docks, probably mid-1930s. Going clockwise from the bottom left, we have Eastern King, with the coastguard station overlooking West Wharf, and the lifeboat station and slipway. The medium-size vessel (is that an Ellerman Lines funnel?) is on West Wharf, which was 'quayed' in the 1880s, while the entrance to the graving dock (in the Inner Basin) is just visible on the left of the frame. The huge grain silo on West Wharf is conspicuous by its absence - it wasn't completed until 1940. Continuing round to the North Wall of the Inner Basin, at its western (left-hand) end it is lined with warehouses - these were gutted in the raids of 1941. The running line to West Wharf lies behind the warehouses. The quayside buildings stand roughly in front of what was once a quarry - the larger buildings near the open space are the flour mills and the laundry (with the chimney), and behind the laundry is East Street school. Stonehouse Town Hall is just to the left while, at the very top of the photograph, is the Royal Naval Hospital. In the extreme upper right-hand corner of the photograph is Millbay station, the route of the dock line (alongside the northlight-roofed warehouse) being discernible.

Barbican Quay, undated. The quay, on the west side of Sutton Harbour, was a focal point for the once-busy Plymouth fishing industry. By the early 1800s some 200 locals were already employed, but after the introduction of trawling circa 1815 the industry boomed. As early as 1820 there were thirty trawlers based at Sutton Harbour, and by 1850 there were around sixty. Although the quay was not rail connected, the improved communications provided by the railways opened up new markets for locally-landed fish, although that was partly at the expense of fishing ports in West Cornwall. By 1930 there were over a hundred boats working out of Sutton Harbour; most of them by then steam vessels, but the last sailing trawler at the harbour didn't cease work until 1938.

Chapter 5
Maritime Matters

'...Plymouth only requires improved Harbour accommodation to maintain, incontestably, the position of the first port of the British Channel.'

The Great Western Dock Co was incorporated in 1846 and, partly in view of possible competition from a LSWR-backed scheme for improving Sutton Harbour, the three broad gauge companies - the SDR, GWR and Bristol & Exeter - subscribed to the dock company. The plan was described by the dock company in 1851: '*A Floating dock or Basin about Thirteen Acres in area, having gates capable of admitting the largest vessels, and giving an extent of wharfage about three-quarters of a mile in length. Within the basin will be a graving dock 330 feet in length. A considerable addition will also be made to the wharfage in the outer harbour, which will be in many parts deepened and otherwise improved.*

'*The selection of Plymouth as the Port for the arrival and departure of the Cape Mail Packets, the preference awarded to it by the Eastern Steam Navigation Company, and more recently by Her Majesty's Commissioners of Emigration, are facts widely known, and have been made the subject of general comment. They sufficiently prove that Plymouth only requires improved Harbour accommodation to maintain, incontestably, the position of the first port of the British Channel'.*

In 1850 the dock company's railway lines were connected to the SDR station at Millbay, and as the years progressed the corporate connections between dock company and the three broad gauge concerns - the 'Associated Companies' - increased. Somewhat predictably, the dock and the three railway companies even shared the same engineer - Isambard Kingdom Brunel.

Some of Brunel's correspondence still survives. In his role as dock engineer, he wrote to the secretary of the dock company on 16 November 1857 on the subject of repairs to the foreshore, the outer pier and the dams, which had suffered storm damage: '*I have no reason to doubt that the directors are using their best endeavours to obtain the means of effecting the Works of Repair, which I stated in my Report of October 24th to be <u>absolutely necessary</u>, and even if the simple and therefore strong term "absolutely necessary" used in that Report did not convey to them all that I intended it should, my letter of the 9th instant must surely have made them feel that I considered that we were incurring, daily and hourly, a fearful risk, by reason of the omission to repair in any way the damage done in the late storm'.* The great man was

clearly in poor mood. The cost of repairs, incidentally, was estimated to be £10,650, and Brunel also recommended that the timber-work at the end of Millbay Pier be replaced by masonry.

Plymouth Docks did reasonable business, but the need for the constant upgrading of facilities proved to be a huge drain on the corporate coffers. Nevertheless, the dock company was quite adept at blowing its own trumpet, as this general announcement of July 1871 indicates:

'*The Pontoon is a floating receptacle capable of containing about 3,000 tons of Coal, and Vessels take in their supplies alongside by day or night, afloat at any time of the tide.*

'*Fresh Water when required is run on board from the Dock company's Pipes, while the Vessel is coaling, at 2/- per tun of 4 hogsheads or 250 Gallons.*

'*The Port Charges are only One Shilling per Vessel and the Dock dues on Vessels calling for Coal One halfpenny per register Ton.*

'*Large stocks of Nixon's Navigation, Newcastle, Wyndham Merthyr, Old Llantwit and other Coals and Patent Fuel are kept on hand, and put free on*

Barbican Fish Market, undated. The market was completed in 1896 and this picture, maybe, was taken not too long after opening day. Other clues as to the date might be gleaned from the registration marks on the vessels, and the fact that there are at least three steam trawlers present. The various fashions, poses and expressions of the assembled throng don't exactly create a welcoming atmosphere - it would have taken a brave man to pick an argument with this lot.

Millbay Jetty, undated. The tender P.S.CHESHIRE (registered at Liverpool) is being unloaded, the mail bags being carried manually to an Ocean Mail train with a '1076' class 0-6-0ST at its head. The carriages appear to be the special Ocean Mail vans (diagram M10), five of which were built in 1903/04; although displaced by new stock in 1928 they lasted until 1950s.

board by the Representatives of the respective Proprietors'.

The dock company nonetheless found itself in an uphill struggle. This caused concern among the Associated Companies, especially the SDR which, doing good business at the docks, was painfully aware of the LSWR's impending presence in the Plymouth area. The GWR conceded that on completion of the standard gauge it must 'expect a more active competition' with the South Western. both for rail and dock traffic. This, it would be 'desirable to meet' by providing 'all possible facilities at the Docks for the speedy discharge and loading of Vessels'. On 12 May 1873 the SDR General Manager, L.J. Seargeant, prepared a report on the docks for the Associated Companies. It not only detailed proposed improvements to the docks but, significantly, also set out a case for a joint purchase of the dock company. Improvements would involve the reclamation of considerable quantities of land, and make available wharage which could 'not otherwise be so profitably employed as it might.' The reasons in favour of acquiring the property appeared, to Seargeant, thus: *'That Parliamentary power to do so exists.*

'That assuming the desirability of purchase no better opportunity than the

Plymouth Sound, undated. Mails being loaded on to the GWR tender P.S.CHESHIRE in Plymouth Sound.

Plymouth Sound, undated. When reference is made to the GWR ocean liner traffic at Plymouth Docks, it must be remembered that the large liners didn't actually enter the docks. The vessels berthed in Plymouth Sound, and passengers and mail were transferred to a railway-owned tender which took them to the docks. Here, the tender is the P.S.CHESHIRE, the photograph presumably being taken from another of the tenders. Was this a case of a substantial loading of passengers and mails (a requirement for two tenders) or simply a photographic excursion to record the CHESHIRE in action? This landlubber of a scribe was tempted to suggest that the activity seen here might have been connected with the much-publicised run from the R.M.S.MAURETANIA in 1924. However, it has been emphasised in no uncertain terms that the R.M.S.MAURETANIA was not the only liner with four funnels.

present is likely to present itself.
'That by a comparatively small outlay valuable Land may be reclaimed and the Outer Harbour may be made available for Ocean Steamers - no accommodation now existing for them at Plymouth.
'That when the South Western are at Plymouth, separate management at the Docks may be inconvenient.
'That the Docks being in the market, it would be more inconvenient if the South Western had them - by themselves or their Allies.
'That the Property may now be purchased by arrangements involving

small sacrifice to the Company or Companies buying.
'That the Traffic Receipts shew sure and satisfactory increase from time to time.
' That the Dock Company if left to themselves will not have sufficient resources to carry out improvements of great importance to the Companies' interests'.

The report summarised the financial state of play - shares were held in the proportion Great Western £19,520, Bristol & Exeter £30,030 and South Devon £56,270. Receipts had been as:

	No of vessels	Tonnage	£
1868	2,016	421,137	14,013
1869	2,059	443,165	14,918
1870	2,079	410,947	15,143
1871	2,373	399,484	15,837
1872	2,441	453,869	17,547

The expenses for 1872 were £7,116, which gave a profit of £10,431.

In 1874 the Associated Companies took over the Great Western Docks, the GWR assuming total control two years later when it absorbed the SDR and B&ER. In 1876 the GWR proposed £100,000 of improvements to the docks and although the overall scheme was deferred, some improvements were undertaken. A new wharf on the western side of the outer basin was constructed, dredged to a depth of 24ft and provided with steam cranes and hoists. Warehouse accommodation was increased, and cattle sheds and a slaughterhouse were provided on the new West Wharf.

A report on the progress with the West Wharf works was made by Brunel's successor, Peter Marjary, on 1 January 1880 - a timber wharf in front of the concrete walls had been completed, two-thirds of the excavation for the boat basin has been done, a road for the Admiralty was finished and the outer jetty was 'about half done'. Two warehouses, with verandah, a line along the Admiralty retaining wall known as 'The Back Siding' and two lines with loop and connections to the new wharf were all complete. 'Practically a

Liner movements at Plymouth, October 1882

16

ARRANGEMENTS FOR THE
ARRIVAL OF
MAIL AND PASSENGER SHIPS AT PLYMOUTH

Oct.	Ports of Destination.	SHIP.	OWNERS.
1	New York	Westphalia	Hamburg-American s.s. Co
2	Madeira, C. of G. Hope,& Natal	Asiatic	Union Steamship Co., Lim
3	China	Shannon	P. & O. Steam Nav. Co.
3	Calcutta and Bombay	Assam	P. and O. Steam Nav. Co.
4	Sydney, Melbourne, & Adelaide	Chimborazo	Orient Line.
6	New York	Frisia	Hamburg-American s.s. Co
9	Australia	Almora	Queens'nd Royal Mail Line
10	Australia and Bombay	Ravenna	P. and O. Steam Nav. Co.
10	Cape Town and Madeira	Grantully Castle	Castle Mail Packet Co.
12	West Indies	Don	Royal Mail Steam Packet Co
13	Madeira, C. of G. Hope, & Natal	German	Union Steamship Co.
15	New York	Herder	Hamburg-American s.s. Co
17	Madeira,C. of G. Hope,& Natal,	Moor	Union Steamship Co., Lim.
17	Australia	Rome	P. and O. Steam Nav. Co.
22	Sydney, Melbourne & Adelaide	John Elder	Orient Line
22	New York	Gellert	Hamburg-American s.s. Co
24	C. Town, St. Helena, Ascension and Madeira	Drummond Castle	Castle Mail Packet Co.
25	China and Bombay	Thibet	P. and O. Steam Nav. Co.
26	West Indies	Moselle	Royal Mail Steam Packet Co.
29	New York	Suevia	Hamburg-American s.s. Co.
30	Madeira, C. of G. Hope,& Natal	Athenian	Union Steamship Co., Lim.

LOCAL AGENTS FOR THE MAIL AND PASSENGER SHIPS—Continued.

Royal Mail Steam Packet Co.
Peninsular & Oriental S. N'gt. Co.
Direct Line
} Fox, Sons, & Co., Hoegate Street, Plymouth.

Australian & New Zealand s'g ships
South African Line of Steamers
Queensland Royal Mail Line
Colonial Line to Australia
British India Steam Navigtn. Co.
} Weekes, Phillips, & Co. Barbican, Plymouth.

The Company does not hold itself responsible for the correctness of these
S₁ ll'', though every care is taken to procure it.

17

ARRANGEMENTS FOR THE
DEPARTURE OF
MAIL AND PASSENGER SHIPS FROM PLYMOUTH

Oct.	SAILING TO.	SHIP.	OWNERS.
1	Cherbourg and Hamburg	Westphalia	Hamburg-American s.s. Co.
3	Sydney	Paramatta, slg. sh.	Devitt and Moore
3	Madeira, C. of G. Hope, & Natal	Durban	Union Steamship Co., Lim.
8	Cherbourg and Hamburg	Frisia	Hamburg-American s.s. Co.
9	Melbourne and Sydney	Potosi	Orient Line
11	Queensland Ports	Albany	Queens'nd Royal Mail Line
12	Cape Colonies	Cotherstone	South African Line
13	Cherbourg and Southampton	Don	Royal Mail SteamPacket Co.
14	Madeira, C. of G. Hope, & Natal	A steamer	Union Steamship Co., Lim.
14	Rockhampton	Melpomene sg.sh.	McIlwraith, McEachern&Co
15	Cherbourg and Hamburg	Herder	Hamburg-American s.s. Co.
16	Sydney	Euterpe,slg. ship	Shaw, Savill, and Co.
20	Madeira, C. of G. Hope, & Natal	Spartan	Union Steamship Co., Lim.
20	Adelaide, Melbourne & Sydney	Aberdeen	G. Thompson and Co
21	Melbourne	Chimborazo	Orient Line
22	Cherbourg and Hamburg	Gellert	Hamburg-American s.s. Co.
23	Queensland Ports	Merkara	Queens'nd Royal Mail Line
23	Cape Colonies	A steamer	South African Line
25	Adelaide	Torrens,slg. ship	Trinder, Anderson & Co.
28	Cherbourg and Southampton	Moselle	Royal Mail Steam Packet Co.
28	Madeira, C. of G. Hopa,& Natal	Asiatic	Union Steamship Co
29	Cherbourg and Hamburg	Suevia	Hamburg-American s.s. Co.
30	Adelaide	Arthurstone (slg. ship)	D. Bruce and Co.

LOCAL AGENTS FOR THE MAIL AND PASSENGER SHIPS.

British & African Steam Nav. Co.
African Steamship Company
Union Steamship Co., Limited
West African Steam Navigat'n Co
} Henry J. Waring & Co., Millbay, Plymouth.

Hamburg-American Company
Castle Mail Packets s.s. Co.
} Smith, Sundius, & Co., Millbay Road, Plymo.

Money Wigram & Sons to Australia
Orient Line
Hoult Line
} J. T. Wright, & Co., Duke of Cornwall Buildings.

Official SDR plan of Plymouth Docks, pre-1876

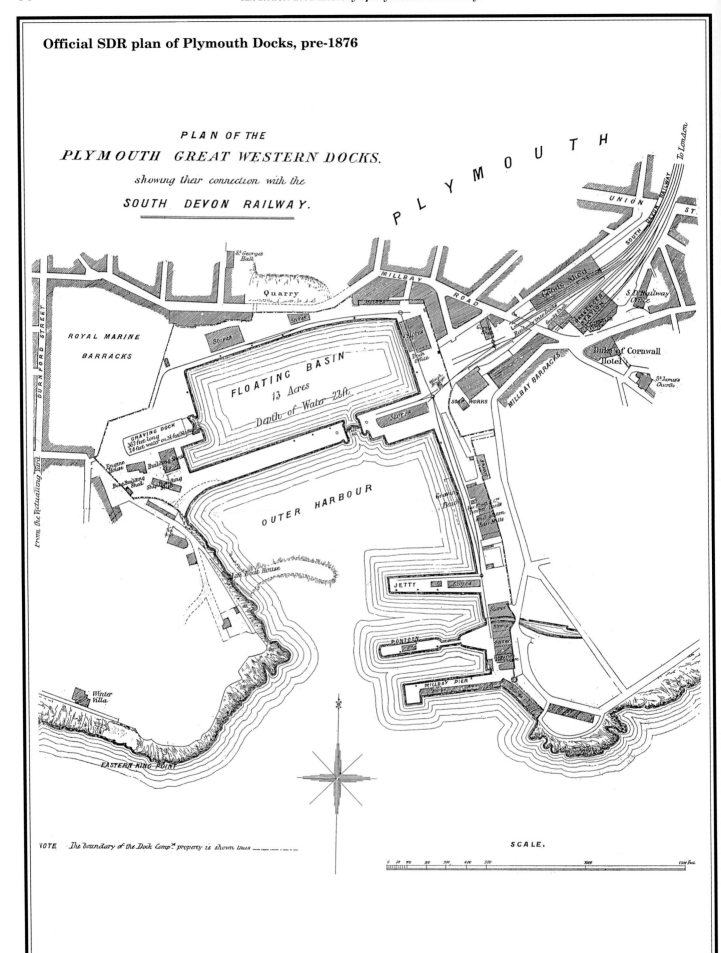

PLAN OF THE

PLYMOUTH GREAT WESTERN DOCKS.

showing their connection with the

SOUTH DEVON RAILWAY.

PLYMOUTH

St Georges Hall

Quarry

ROYAL MARINE BARRACKS

DURNFORD STREET

Stores

from the Victualling Yard

GRAVING DOCK
367 feet long
24 feet water on Sheet Ledge

Engine House

Boat Building Shed

Ship Building

Building Shed

FLOATING BASIN
13 Acres
Depth of Water 22ft.

Stores

Dock Office

Wash House

Stores

OUTER HARBOUR

Life Boat House

JETTY

Stores

PONTOON

Stores

Stores

MILLBAY PIER

Stores

Winter Villa

EASTERN KING POINT

MILLBAY ROAD

Stores

Goods Shed

Railway in the Dock

Goods Shed

Goods Shed

Goods Hall

PASSENGER STATION

S.D. Railway Office

SOUTH DEVON RAILWAY

UNION ST.

To London

MILLBAY BARRACKS

SOAP WORKS

Timber Yards
and Steam Saw Mills

Duke of Cornwall Hotel

St James's Church

NOTE. The boundary of the Dock Compy property is shown thus _____

SCALE.

0 50 100   200   300   400   500   1000   1500 Feet

GWR Ocean Liner Terminal, April 1927. A mail train, headed by a GWR 4-6-0, prepares to depart from Millbay. Three mail coaches and a bogie clerestory, alongside which is a '1361' class 0-6-0ST, wait on the quayside. The GWR tender, SIR WALTER RALEIGH, is alongside Trinity Pier. In the distance - seemingly on the horizon but actually only two miles distant - is Plymouth Breakwater. Started in 1812 and finished circa 1844 at a cost of around £1,500,000, the breakwater consumed some 3.5 million tons of stone, some of which came from quarries at Oreston. PHOTOGRAPH: WELSH INDUSTRIAL & MARITIME MUSEUM

commencement was made yesterday' Marjary continued, when 130 tons of mixed goods were 'expeditiously shipped' from wagons on the new wharf to the *Sir Francis Drake*, 'for one of the Orient Steam Ship company's boats for Australia, lying in the Sound'.

By 1881 the annual trade at the docks was worth almost £30,000 - though in 1879 the figure had actually reached over £35,000. The bad news was that, between 1871 and 1881, the working expenses had risen from 43% of receipts to 60%. The expenses for 1880 had, however, included £5,073, compensation paid for damage to the *Shadivan* which had struck a rock in the outer basin.

Despite the LSWR's entry into Plymouth in 1876 and the laying of mixed gauge rails to Millbay (thereby giving the LSWR access to the Great Western Docks) in 1878, by the early 1880s almost 92% of Plymouth's rail-borne maritime trade was still handled by the GWR. The limited nature of LSWR trade at the Great Western Docks was due partly to an arrangement whereby its locomotives did not work to or within the docks, the traffic being exchanged at North Road station. Nevertheless, during the 1880s the LSWR took some 80% of the emigrant traffic *from* London *to* Plymouth. The GWR suspected an 'arrangement' with the Emigration Agent at London (the emigrants travelled via Cattewater) but this could not be proved.

The GWR kept a close watch on the LSWR, particularly when the latter was making headway with its branch to Stonehouse Pool, and LSWR involvement with the Cattewater branch also came under Great Western scrutiny. The Cattewater branch actually belonged to the horse-worked Plymouth & Dartmoor Railway, and although the SDR was empowered to demand that the branch be built to accept broad gauge rails, the P&DR refused to have any dealings with the SDR. The South Devon eventually conceded that the trade it was likely to obtain at Cattewater was not worth the expense of laying broad gauge rails, and did not pursue its case.

The P&DR subsequently entered into an agreement with the LSWR, and so the latter finished up with three maritime outlets in the Plymouth area: Stonehouse Pool, Cattewater, and Sutton Harbour. The last-named was also served by the GWR, albeit by a completely separate branch.

In September 1882 the GWR prepared a report on its ocean liner trade:

'The Company's steam tenders meet every Vessel on arrival at Plymouth, and convey the Passengers and their baggage to the Docks.

'Formerly, passengers arriving by the Ocean Vessels had either to walk or take a cab to the Railway Station, but now, whenever the Vessels disembark their passengers by daylight, and in sufficient numbers, railway carriages

and luggage vans are placed opposite the Custom House at the Docks, so that after clearing their luggage, passengers can take their seats and be conveyed to London or to any other Station at which the train may stop, via Millbay Station, without change of Carriage, and the Custom House and the Waiting Rooms have been enlarged, and separate accommodation provided, for third class passengers.

'The arrangement for the conveyance of passengers from the Docks, by Railway, was commenced on the arrival at the Port of Plymouth of the first Peninsular & Oriental Company's homeward-bound vessels in January 1882, and in the first instance was for the special convenience of the P&O passengers, that Company having determined to make Plymouth a regular port of call. The facility has, however, now been extended to the Union, Royal Mail, Castle, and Orient Steamship Companies when their Steamers arrive at a favourable time for the day trains, and land a sufficient number of passengers'.

The incentives offered to steamship passengers by the GWR included the advance issue of coupons (to avoid the need for re-booking for the train journey), a reduction of about one-third in the fares to London, and a 100% increase in the luggage allowance on the trains.

The GWR had the ocean liner traffic at Plymouth all to itself until 1904, when the LSWR opened its new passenger terminal at Stonehouse Pool. The branch thence from Devonport had opened to goods traffic in 1886, a single track line diverging from the main line on the approach to Devonport station, and dropping sharply to pass underneath the goods yard before continuing to the waterfront. When the American Line decided that its ships should call at Plymouth *en route* to Southampton, the LSWR promptly upgraded the branch for passenger traffic and built a well-equipped terminal at Stonehouse Pool.

At the terminal, the LSWR rented space from the Stonehouse Pool Improvement Co. The terms were £200 per annum for two years from the date of first occupation 'with an additional payment of 2d per head for each excursion passenger, 6d for each ocean passenger, inclusive of personal baggage, and 1ˆd per ton for coal for the use of the tender'.

Passenger business at Stonehouse Pool commenced on 9 April 1904, when the *S.S. St.Louis* arrived at Plymouth Sound. The first LSWR 'Ocean Liner' train from Plymouth was hauled by 'S11' class 4-4-0 No 399 and, apparently, it covered the distance to Exeter, a little over 56 miles, in just over 60 minutes. For the services, the LSWR introduced sets of 'Ocean Special' carriages, some six inches wider than ordinary carriages and considerably more luxurious. Each set had sleeping cars - the only ones on the LSWR -

complete with brass bedsteads. The coaches were sold to the GWR in 1911, after the LSWR had withdrawn its Ocean Liner services from Stonehouse Pool, and one survived in GWR stock until 1931.

In May 1907 the White Star Line (another of the LSWR's clients) also started calling at Plymouth *en route* to Southampton, but things were, by then, looking a little grim for the railway company. Just three months earlier, the American Line ship, the *S.S. New York*, had disembarked only eleven passengers at Plymouth. Of those, just three took the boat train to Waterloo.

The LSWR's ocean liner traffic at Stonehouse Pool lasted only until 1910 and, two years later, the roof of the the Ocean Liner Terminal was removed. Nevertheless, this embarrassingly brief foray into the ocean passenger market at Plymouth attracted other worthwhile business to the Stonehouse Pool area, some of which survived in one form or another for around half a century. It was more prosaic stuff, but business all the same. In November 1905, for example, the LSWR Traffic Committee reported that the Homelight Oil Company and the General Petroleum Company proposed to establish oil depots near the Stonehouse Pool branch at Richmond Walk; they required permission to lay a line of pipes from the Quay at Stonehouse Pool Station to the depots, and to be provided with a siding. The LSWR agreed, stipulating a charge of £1 per chain per

annum for the pipes passing its property plus £25 per annum for the ground occupied by the siding. The cost of laying the siding (estimated at £800) was to be borne by the oil companies, who also had to foot the bill for maintaining the connections.

During the Southern Railway era, the activities at Stonehouse Pool usually warranted only the occasional brief paragraph in the Docks and Marine Committee minutes. Random examples from the mid-1920s reveal the everyday routine: the letting of premises at Stonehouse Pool for curing and packing of herrings, 'for a limited period at a rent of £240 per annum, plus rates and taxes' in 1924 and the re-equipping of the quays - two new steam cranes 'to bring them up to modern requirements' in 1926. On the staff front, SR minutes of 5 October 1927 refer to the retirement of the Stonehouse Pool general foreman, Mr T. Williams, a month or so before his seventieth birthday: '*He was taken over from the Stonehouse Pool Improvement Company on 1st July 1907 when the South Western Company acquired the quay. He has carried out his duties in a very satisfactory manner, in view of which it is recommended that a special retiring allowance of 10/- weekly be granted, not to be subject to reduction in the customary way upon receipt of the Government Old Age Pension, and that a retiring gratuity of £50 be made to him*'.

As far as the Plymouth ocean liner traffic was concerned, it was, of course,

Millbay Level Crossing, circa 1914. The railway crosses Millbay Road on the level - the station is to the right and the docks to the left. Note the gas lamps, even on the footbridge. **PHOTOGRAPH: WELSH INDUSTRIAL & MARITIME MUSEUM**

Millbay Level Crossing, circa 1914. Single line working is in operation while fairly extensive repairs are being undertaken to the down line between Millbay station and the docks. The roof of Millbay station is discernible behind the unidentified 0-6-0ST.
PHOTOGRAPH: WELSH INDUSTRIAL & MARITIME MUSEUM

the GWR's role which is best remembered. At times it seemed as if the independent railway press were acting as publicists, *The Railway Magazine* of November 1897, for example, celebrated the arrival of the North German Lloyd Company's new steamer *'Kaiser Wilhelm der Grosse'* from New York, at 3.5pm on October

6th. The special dining car train 'run for the conveyance of passengers' had a record journey, leaving Plymouth at 4.58pm and arriving at Paddington at 9.51pm, 'covering the 247 miles, including two stops, in 4 hours 53 minutes'. The complete journey from New York to London was accomplished (the GW leg seemed the most important

part, to *The Railway Magazine*) in less than six days, 'using the GWR route which is, we believe, impossible by any other route'.

The GWR's own organ, the *GWR Magazine*, regularly reported on maritime activities at Plymouth. Here's a random selection, starting with the issue for January 1908: *'A record*

Millbay Pier, circa 1911. The small narrow gauge wagons transferred baggage from the tenders to the Customs Hall via a circular track. **PHOTOGRAPH: WELSH INDUSTRIAL & MARITIME MUSEUM5**

Millbay station and quays, taken from the 25in Ordnance Survey map of 1914. Crown Copyright.

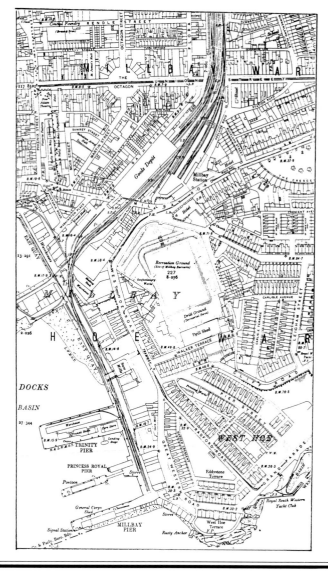

The last sentence in that account did more than a little to confirm the GWR - LSWR rivalry. It also evidenced another GWR 'victory'. Earlier, the LSWR had applied to the Post Office to carry the mails from the White Star Line and American Line ships, but the application had been rejected and the GWR continued to handle the business. It also transported the gold bullion which was carried by the liners.

In February 1908 the *GWR Magazine* reported that two additional lines were to commence regular services into Plymouth: the Royal Mail Steam Packet Company with vessels from Cuba and Mexico and Lund's Blue Anchor Line, with steamers plying between Australia, South Africa and England. Sixty two ocean liners were listed to embark or disembark passengers during the month of May, the magazine reported. This reportage continued across the years, for these ships represented the high glamour of the transport world. In June 1933 for instance, the GWR house magazine celebrated the arrival of the United States new liner *'Washington'*, making Plymouth her first port of call on its maiden voyage from New York to England, with the newly appointed United States Ambassador to Great Britain and his family among the passengers. The ship landed 135 passengers for London on May 17, and a special train left Plymouth Docks for Paddington. The Great Western docks were decorated with British and American flags, and the Mayor and other civic officers visited the ship during her stay at Plymouth.

Business was prodigious as the 1930s wore on - on July 5 1934, as the worst effects of the Slump began to subside, the largest number of American visitors ever landed at Plymouth in one day, 1,300,

consignment of mails, consisting of 3,251 bags, was landed at the Great Western Docks on the arrival of the White Star Liner "Oceanic" on December 24th (1907). Two tenders were provided for the mails, and 38 minutes after their arrival at the Docks the whole of the bags were transferred to the special train, the journey to Paddington occupying 4 hours 19 minutes. A separate tender was provided for the passengers, of whom 99 were landed and conveyed by special trains to Bristol and Paddington, the latter point being reached in 4 hours 28 minutes.

'The American liner "Philadelphia" arrived at Plymouth on the morning of December 18th, and landed passengers and 1,460 bags of mails. A special train left Plymouth at 11.45am and reached Paddington at 4.5pm, the London & South Western special (for the passengers) reaching Waterloo at 5.30pm'.

Millbay Quay, April 1927. The 'modern electric belt conveyor', seemingly almost new in this official record shot, was installed to facilitate the unloading of mails and baggage from the tenders to the trains. A welcome advantage of the conveyor was that it could be lowered to deck-level, no matter what the state of the tide.
PHOTOGRAPH: WELSH INDUSTRIAL & MARITIME MUSEUM

Millbay Quay, April 1927. Another official picture of the 'electric belt conveyor'. Fortunately for posterity, if there were any innovation on the GWR - no matter how trivial it seemed to mere mortals - an official photographer was despatched to take pictures from almost every conceivable angle. The SIR WALTER RALEIGH was one of the Plymouth tenders, the original vessel (of 1876) being replaced by one of the same name in the late 1920s/early 1930s. Also around that time, two new tenders appeared on the scene - the SIR RICHARD GRENVILLE and the SIR JOHN HAWKINS. PHOTOGRAPH: WELSH INDUSTRIAL & MARITIME MUSEUM

disembarked from the ocean liners 'Leviathan', 'Paris', 'Colombia', 'Columbus' and 'Statenham'. Five special boat expresses were run from Plymouth to Paddington conveying the passengers, their baggage, and Post Office mails.

By November 1937 the total imports and exports at the Millbay Docks amounted to 218,295 tons, though this had to be set against the 223,486 tons of the corresponding period in 1936, the decrease being mainly due to a falling off in the imports of grain and flour for cattle feeding purposes. By November 14th, 425 homeward and 31 outward bound calls were made by ocean liners at Plymouth, and 32,146 passengers and 162,060 bags of mails were landed and embarked. Among the notable vessels calling were the Cunard liner 'Queen Mary' and the French liner 'Normandie'. The season for the import of French fruit lasted from May 28th to June 18th, and during this period no less than thirty-three vessels arrived at Plymouth to discharge *1,318 tons* of strawberries, a staggering figure 112 tons in excess of the 1936 season.

On April 11th 1938, the magazine recorded, the Cunard-White Star R.M.S. 'Queen Mary' made her first call of the season at Plymouth. The giant liner arrived in Cawsand Bay at 9.0am and the Great Western's fleet of four tenders put out to disembark 300 passengers and 537 bags of mail. Two special trains

were run from Plymouth Docks to Paddington, at 12.11pm and 12.52pm.

Apart from this sort of in-house *Company Notes,* the GWR was notable for the alacrity with which the publicity people fixed upon any weapons in the PR campaign. A *Ports and Harbours* book was published each year, mainly as a sales pitch for prospective customers, and the 1934 edition boasted: *'The Company's tenders - first-class steamers maintained in the*

highest state of efficiency and general condition - run between the docks and the great ocean liners anchored in the sound, and on reaching the Dock are berthed on the north side of Millbay Pier. Mails are dealt with by a modern electric belt conveyor, and the Company have recently erected an electric travelling crane of 25cwt capacity, in order to deal more expeditiously with passengers' heavy baggage. Adjoining the pier are spacious waiting and refreshment rooms and baggage examination halls, from alongside which the express trains depart.

'North of the Millbay Pier, and on the eastern side of the Outer Dock, there is a very fine floating pontoon, which is available as an extra landing place for passengers and mails. From here also the company's steamers run passenger trips in the summer season to the many points of beauty and historic interest for which Plymouth is such a convenient centre'.

'Trinity Pier, a jetty of solid construction, is equipped with transit sheds. At this pier is handled the extensive traffic with the Continental ports in fruit and general goods. On the opposite side of the Outer Dock is the west wharf, 750 feet in length, providing deep-water berths for the largest cargo steamers, and equipped with first-class hydraulic cranes and commodious transit sheds. Here, many of the valuable cargoes of grain brought from South America, Canada etc are discharged'.

A rather different insight into maritime activities at Plymouth came in the *GWR Magazine* of April 1938, under the title *On a Plymouth Tender:*

'Three sharp blasts from the siren, a clang of the bell from the bridge, and the GWR tender "Sir Walter Raleigh" glides slowly from Millbay Dock. It is

West Wharf, September 1924. Cargo for the Midlands and the North is discharged. Note the original ownership of the LMSR wagons. PHOTOGRAPH: WELSH INDUSTRIAL & MARITIME MUSEUM

East Quay, September 1924. The building with the clock is the dock office. PHOTOGRAPH: WELSH INDUSTRIAL & MARITIME MUSEUM

eight o'clock of a perfect spring evening, and there is hardly a ripple on the waters, as, with increasing speed we make our way towards the breakwater - that long, protecting arm which affords the necessary shelter to the Plymouth Sound.

'Out of the darkness we suddenly see a series of ordered fairy lights, and as we reach the breakwater the lights take shape dimly revealing the American liner, S.S. "Manhattan", riding at anchor and awaiting our arrival. As we draw alongside, ropes are exchanged and we are made fast. Suddenly a large hole appears in the side of the ship. Gangways are hoisted; cranes lean over high above the decks, and the operation of transfer commences. Those of us who have come to bid welcome to the great ship are allowed to ascend the gangway and go aboard. We anticipate confusion but are disappointed.

'An army of white-coated stewards, commanded by that important

Looking across to West Wharf, April 1927. Eastern Kings coastguard station is the most prominent building in the West Wharf area, but thirteen years later that honour, if can be called such, was taken by a new grain silo. PHOTOGRAPH: WELSH INDUSTRIAL & MARITIME MUSEUM

Right:- Millbay Quay, 2 July 1953. A fully-fledged boat train pulls away for Paddington at 9pm. The engines are No.7815 FRITWELL MANOR and No.4088 DARTMOUTH CASTLE, and the train includes at least two of the special saloons built in 1928 to replace the older 'Dreadnought' stock of 1904. Just in front of the leading engine (and out of view) the line curves towards Millbay station. The sidings in the foreground were taken out of use in 1963, but the 'main' line remained until September 1971 - three months after the cessation of rail services to the docks. PHOTOGRAPH: ALAN LATHEY

Millbay Level Crossing, 1 May 1954. A London-bound special from the S.S.ANTILLES, with No 7824 IFORD MANOR piloting No.7033 HARTLEBURY CASTLE, approaches the crossing. 'Castles' were preferred on these duties for they could work into the docks - if a 'King' were used, a shunting engine had to bring the train from the quayside to the crossing. That said, a 'King' was used for a Coronation Day special in 1953, albeit with only five or six coaches. PHOTOGRAPH: ALAN LATHEY

Passengers are being courteously shepherded towards the customs sheds, and in the background we see a Great Western Ocean express which will in four hours convey them safely and in comfort to Paddington.

'The newsreel apparatus, batteries of cameras, and the excitement of the shore crowd arouses curiosity. A whisper goes round "the American Ambasador is on board". Film stars and other celebrities are keenly watched by their fans.

'All this has taken place in less than two hours, and although it is a regular occurrence and smooth in its efficiency, it is not without its thrill'.

Inevitably, the Second World War made for a major hiatus in the ocean liner traffic, but things gradually returned to normal after 1945. On 9 July 1949 a British Railways Working Party visited Plymouth to study and report on the disembarkation of 215

personage, the baggage master, stand by, and at the word of command attack in an energetic but orderly manner a literal mountain of hand luggage. Then, a continuous stream of luggage goes down the gangway to the deck of the tender.

'While this operation is in progress two other tenders have arrived, and a glance at the other side of the ship shows us the discharge of cars, heavy luggage and mails.

'The four hundred passengers who are landing at Plymouth are lined up before the purser and his assistants. Familiar sounds are heard: "Get your landing cards ready, please". Leave is taken of new-found friends and the stream of passengers descends the gangway.

'When all is ready we quietly glide away from the sides of the ship and turn our eyes to the lights of Plymouth. Ten minutes sees us safely docked.

Above:- Sutton Harbour, 1 June 1953. Although all but twenty of the 140 GWR '2021' class 0-6-0PTs became BR stock, few made it past the mid-1950s. No.2097 - which succeeded fellow No.2148 as the regular Sutton Harbour engine - itself succumbed in March 1955. It is seen shunting at the coal wharf at Coxside, the unloading gantries being clearly visible in the background. 'Red' group engines (except 'Castles' and '47XXs') were nominally permitted to work the Sutton Harbour branch as far as Sutton Road level crossing gates, but only 'Uncoloured' engines were allowed past the crossing. Most of the lines at Sutton Harbour had been taken out of use by December 1972. PHOTOGRAPH: ALAN LATHEY

Left:- Veteran '2021' class 0-6-0PT No.2038 shunts near Northey's Sidings on the Sutton Harbour branch, 2 April 1952. - note the cleanliness of the engine on this humble duty. PHOTOGRAPH: ALAN LATHEY

Sutton Harbour lines - with the LSWR branch from Friary just discernible in the top of the frame. 25in Ordnance Survey map of 1914. Crown Copyright.

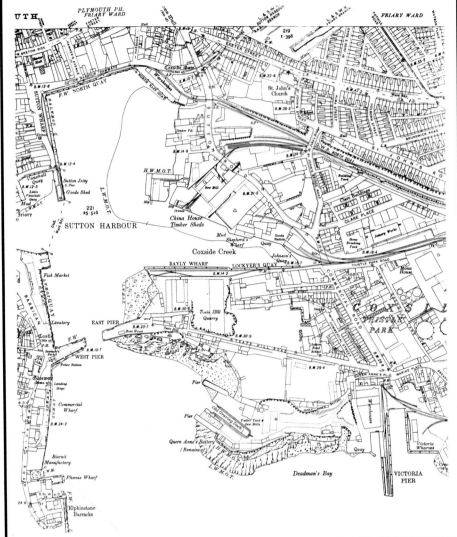

Stonehouse Pool, 1 March 1952. 'O2' 0-4-4T No.30216 prepares to depart from the quay at Stonehouse Pool - it is hard to believe that this neglected spot once accommodated the LSWR's Ocean Liner terminal. The remaining buildings on the quayside had been gutted in the 1941 air raids. PHOTOGRAPH: ALAN LATHEY

passengers from the 'S.S. *Marine Tiger*', a former troop ship which had been converted for the tourist market. The Working Party confirmed the importance of Plymouth as 'a tourist port', a fact demonstrated by the regular calls of ships throughout the season. The Americans were certainly welcome, maybe more than ever; besides 'the wealthier Americans' the BR chaps noted another class of tourist - 'young Americans of the middle income group', who were 'especially welcome'. The beauty of the view from the anchorage, it was felt, and the historical interest of this place, made Plymouth an attactive port to American tourists. Before the war Plymouth had been a popular calling port for liner traffic from America and the Far East, for the landing of mails and passengers. By 1949 the mails had passed the pre-war peak

Stonehouse Pool, 22 April 1954. The branch goods negotiates the level crossing at Richmond Road - a fine picture of an largely ignored aspect of Plymouth's railways. The engine is 'E1R' 0-6-2T No.32095, which had started life as an 0-6-0T but had been rebuilt in 1927. It was transferred from Barnstaple to Plymouth (Friary) in autumn 1953, and was withdrawn in November 1956. PHOTOGRAPH: ALAN LATHEY

Cattedown, 2 April 1952. There were ultimately three rail-connected oil depots - Esso, Conoco and Regent - along the Cattewater branch, hence the frequent manifestation of tank wagons on the line and the use of spark arresters on locomotive chimneys. 'B4' No.30094 pauses between shunting manoeuvres. PHOTOGRAPH: ALAN LATHEY

Top:- Cattedown, 3 February 1951. Treated to its new BR livery and number only the previous month, 'B4' No.30102 shows off its plated-in cab and rectangular windows. The brake van is particularly interesting - note the double doors amidships. A guess has been hazarded that the van carried re-railing equipment, minor derailments being far from uncommon on the sharply-curved and uneven tracks on the Cattewater branch. PHOTOGRAPH: ALAN LATHEY

Above:- Cattedown, 7 March 1951. Five months before being given its BR livery and number, 'B4' No.84 (30084) - the last engine to have been built at Nine Elms works - passes the glue works on the Cattewater branch with Esso empties. On the opposite side of the river, behind the engine, are Oreston Quarries. PHOTOGRAPH: ALAN LATHEY

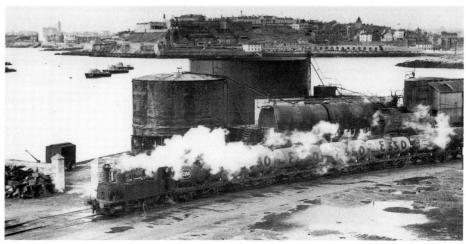

Cattedown, 9 January 1951. Continuing with our photographic exploration of comparatively unrecorded corners of Plymouth, a train of wagons from the Esso premises (near the end of the Cattewater branch) is hauled away by 'B4' 0-4-0T No.84 (soon to be renumbered 30084). The Citadel and Phoenix Wharf can be seen on the far side of Sutton Harbour. PHOTOGRAPH: ALAN LATHEY

The LSWRs Ocean Liner Terminal at Stonehouse Pool was short-lived, but it didn't escape the Ordnance Surveyor in 1907. Taken from the 25in map. Crown Copyright.

figures but the passenger traffic had been slow to recover. 'It may be' the BR Officers suggested, due to the lack of hotel accommodation at Plymouth 'which deters shipping companies from sending traffic to the port'. Despite all the efforts of the Great Western, relatively few passengers had ever embarked at Plymouth; by 1949 the one exception seemed to be the Red Star Line which, under the name of Bernstein & Co, of New York, 'was expected once again to embark as well as to land passengers.' Though this would be 'next year'.

In 1949 plans were already prepared for improvement of the existing facilities, in their nature both short and long term. Those for the short term were under consideration by the Western Region and consisted of restoring the heavily bomb damaged pre-war

Ocean mail and passenger traffic handled at Plymouth 1929–48. The post-war collapse is particularly evident.				
Year	Inward liners	Outward liners	Passengers (in and out)	mails(in and out)
1929	667	77	40,636	317,594
1930	682	106	43,072	307,912
1931	606	101	34,799	222,914
1932	536	86	30,852	226,255
1933	500	92	29,632	207,362
1934	500	96	35,731	213,466
1935	471	33	34,528	233,314
1936	478	20	31,747	206,812
1937	483	32	34,343	201,085
1938	471	29	31,869	166,818
1939	294	38	20,920	81,709
1945	46	-	2,991	43,978
1946	50	6	4,434	135,078
1947	60	6	3,589	112,996
1948	97	12	5,759	355,365

facilities. Long term plans envisaged the complete rebuilding of the accommodation and the resiting of the boat train terminus. The short-term war work was estimated at £15,000, whereas the long term plan was in the neighbourhood of £450,000. The report went on to describe the arrangements for passengers, and made several recommendations for updating the facilities. Passenger access to the boat

Left:- Keyham, 1 March 1952. Seafaring activities out of Plymouth were, of course, not only in the merchant field. The Admiralty has had a presence since 1691 and, throughout much of the railway era, there has inevitably been an exchange of traffic between the Navy and the railway companies. Here, 'O2' No.30216, having satisfied the Admiralty's requirements, pulls away from the Devonport Dockyard branch and on to the GWR line at Keyham. The branch joins the main line just to the north of Keyham station - the connection to the up line (seen alongside one of the rear wagons, and controlled by the 'ground discs on the signal post) was laid in March 1941 but was removed in December 1956. PHOTOGRAPH: ALAN LATHEY

Devonport Dockyard, probably around 1960. The Admiralty - later Ministry of Defence - had its own fleet of locomotives for working at the dockyard itself and latterly, these were 'Planet' diesels, ten of which were purchased new in 1955/56 to replace the remaining steam engines. Here, MoD 'Planet' No.4858 meets WR 0-6-0PT No.9711 at the exchange sidings. PHOTOGRAPH: HUGH DAVIES

trains (from rail level via temporary wooden steps - though it seems primitive now) was not considered a serious disadvantage as 'passengers were protected from the weather by a roofed verandah which runs alongside the train'. The report included a list of the 57 passenger-carrying ships which had called at Plymouth between 1 January and 31 August 1949. Of those, 25 had arrived from New York, the largest being the '*S.S.Ile de France*' of 44,000 grt, although only seven others were over 10,000 tons.

Plymouth's continuing ability to handle boat train traffic was dramatically evidenced in 1957 when, as a result of Southampton's dockers' refusal to handle the '*R.M.S.Queen Mary*', the vessel's passengers were landed at Cherbourg and then

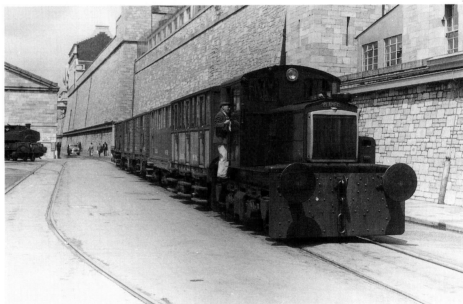

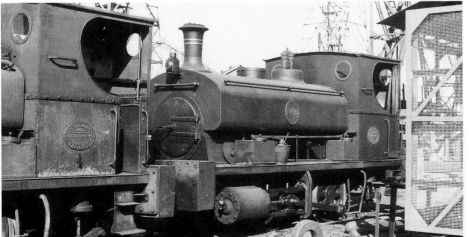

Devonport Dockyard, March 1956. Barclay 0-4-0ST No.10 (Works No.1379) was built in 1914 and scrapped in 1957, displaced by the 'Planet' diesels. PHOTOGRAPH: FRANK JONES

Above:- Devonport Dockyard, around 1960. Such was the extent of the dockyard - some two miles between extremities - that, in 1900, an internal passenger service was introduced on the dockyard railway. The service lasted until May 1966, when road improvements allowed the use of buses, giving a greater measure of flexibility to transport within the dockyard area. The carriages used for the railway service offered no less than six classes of accommodation, the first three (for the higher ranking personnel) having padded seats and, originally, gas lamps, while the other three classes (for Chief Petty Officers and lower ranks) owed more than a little to the 'Parliamentary' style used on Britain's main line railways in the 1840s. This is the internal passenger train, with one of the 'Planet' diesels in charge. PHOTOGRAPH: HUGH DAVIES

Devonport Dockyard, March 1956. Avonside 0-4-0ST No.12 (Works No.1690) of 1915 was also rendered redundant in 1957 by the 'Planet' diesels, but it subsequently had a couple of years' use as a stationary boiler. PHOTOGRAPH: FRANK JONES

transhipped to Plymouth. As there was no time to make new train seating arrangements, the WR borrowed SR boat train sets to convey passengers from Millbay Docks to Paddington. During the frenetic activity at Plymouth on 2 April 1957, the first train of nine Pullmans and five BR bogies (479 tons tare) left Millbay Docks at 8.30pm behind 'Castles' Nos 4077 and 4078, and arrived at Paddington at 12.30am. The second train, loaded to 371 tons and hauled by 'King' No 6025, left Millbay at 10.55pm and arrived at Paddington at 3.19am. The third train, of 423 tons tare, left Millbay at 12.20am behind 'Castle' No 7031 and reached Paddington at 4.57am. Outward-bound passengers travelled to Plymouth in the same stock the following day.

By 1958, the number of liners calling at Plymouth was just 172 for the whole year a far cry from earlier times. In common with other ports, Plymouth's hey-day as a passenger port was long over and business dwindled further during the 1960s. Cessation of the French Line trade in 1961 did little to arrest the decline. The vast social and economic changes of the 1960s effectively brought an end to the exclusivity of international travel - even this writer could afford to travel abroad by aeroplane.

As for freight traffic to and from various British ports, an increasing proportion defected to the roads during the 1950s and 1960s and, furthermore, many ports in the country lost out through an inability to adopt new working practices. The outcome was that the docks and quays at Plymouth, like countless others around the coast of Britain, saw a sharp decline in their freight trade - and much of what remained went by road.

In 1962 - a little more than thirty years ago - 1,401 vessels totalling 304,695 net registered tons used Millbay Docks during the year, total imports being 174,636 tons and exports 2,632 tons. There was still a fair amount of mail traffic from the liners, while much of the freight comprised perishable goods. In the same year, Cattewater Harbour (administered by Cattewater Harbour Commissioners) handled 1,013,865 tons of imports and exports. Much of that was oil and tar, but fertilizer also made a significant contribution. Indeed, the fertilizer traffic warranted one or two block trains to Avonmouth, near Bristol, each week.

The railway line to Millbay was officially closed in July 1971, but the Sutton Harbour branch hung on until December 1973. The Stonehouse Pool branch, for which the old LSWR had once entertained such high hopes, had faded away unnoticed in 1970. It had seen no activity whatsoever since 1966. During the early 1960s, the Stonehouse Pool branch had been served by one or two trains each week; they were usually hauled by an 'O2' 0-4-4T which also undertook daily transfer trips between Devonport (Kings Road) station and Keyham (for the Admiralty yard).

Today, the only former dock line in Plymouth to remain active is the Cattedown spur, but with the cessation of rail traffic to and from the Conoco oil depot at Cattedown a few years ago, only the bitumen traffic remained.

Left:- Devonport Dockyard, 28 September 1951. The narrow-bore tunnel between the North and South Yards at Devonport was, in fact, three separate tunnels in series. It was/they were built in 1854-56 when transport in the dockyards relied on the horse, the first 'real' railway in the dockyard opening in 1867 and extending through the tunnel in 1876. This picture shows the first section of the tunnel (photographed from what is actually known as James Yard) which runs through the substructure of one of the entrance gatehouses. Behind the photographer is the tunnel between North Yard and Morice Yard. When the main tunnel opened, the new form of connection between the two yards marked the end of an era - formerly, the two yards had been regarded as separate entities, each with its own type of duties, working hours and rate of pay. The dockyard continued to expand, partly on reclaimed land, although in the present climate any further expansion of the dockyard seems extremely unlikely. PHOTOGRAPH: FRANK JONES

Chapter Six
The 1950s... and after

After Nationalisation changes soon became evident on much of Britain's railway network, and the Plymouth area was no exception. One early post-Nationalisation loss in the area was the discontinuation of the Plymouth portion of the 'Devon Belle' after the summer of 1949. Another early post-Nationalisation casualty in the Plymouth area was the Turnchapel branch. It was closed temporarily on 2 July 1951 due to the fuel crisis, but although it soon reopened, the reprieve was brief, and passenger services were withdrawn permanently on 10 September. It nevertheless remained open for freight until 2 October 1961 although, in the final years, the traditional Admiralty traffic was negligible. The branch had, for some time, been kept alive largely by domestic coal traffic for Oreston and timber for the private siding east of Turnchapel.

During the 1950s, the changes were duly noted in the contemporary railway press and, arguably, the most comprehensive reporting was found in either the *Railway Observer* or in the pages of *Trains Illustrated*. Much use has made of these records in reconstructing some of the times which follow.

Trains Illustrated correspondents reported as varied a selection as ever. On 8th November 1951, for example, the 3.30pm fromPaddington was in trouble - it was taken on from Newton Abbot by 7804 BAYDON MANOR due to the failure of 7001 SIR JAMES MILNE, and the next day 7914 LLEWENI HALL had to take over from 7024 POWIS CASTLE... 'Stars' were now permitted to work between Exeter and Plymouth over the ex-SR route, and No.4054 had been in regular use on the 2.35pm Plymouth Friary to Exeter Central, returning on the 6.47pm to Plymouth. The working was, in fact, short-lived; the correspondent omitted to mention that 4054 was in abysmal condition and, when climbing up to Exeter Central with a modest three-coach loading, was barely visible through leaking steam!

The New Order was in evidence and of course, remarked upon - Exmouth Junction 2-6-4Ts began working through to Plymouth (Friary) at the end of November 1951 (these were the Fairburn LMSR 2-6-4Ts, four of which were allocated to Exmouth Junction for a short period) whilst the first 'Britannia' to reappear at Laira after modification was 70022 TORNADO, which resumed a turn involving the down 'Cornish Riviera' between Plymouth and Penzance.

Further trials carried out on the South Devon banks with the Metrovick gas turbine No.18100, and the last test runs to Plymouth had included that summer's 'Cornish Riviera', a schedule of four and a half hours. On 30th June 1952, the first day of the summer services, 6008 KING JAMES II brought the down 'Cornish Riviera' into Plymouth four minutes early and on 20th August 1952 a Hereford 'Saint', No. 2920 was seen at Plymouth.

Among the events missed by the *Trains Illustrated* watchers in 1952 was the introduction (in September) of Ivatt 2-6-2Ts on the Bere Alston - Callington services, which were serviced by Friary shed. The arrival of the '2MTs' resulted in the

Mannamead, 15 July 1956. Due to engineering work - a regular occurrence on Sundays - single line working is the order of the day. Consequently, Exmouth Junction Pacific No.34033 CHARD takes the 'wrong' line with a comparatively heavy Plymouth - Waterloo train. PHOTOGRAPH: R.C. RILEY

Devonport (Kings Road) station, 24 October 1951 and Laira 'Star' 4-6-0 No.4054 PRINCESS CHARLOTTE - in dire mechanical condition but nevertheless well-polished despite being only four months away from withdrawal - leaves with the 2.25pm Friary - Exeter stopping train. It is believed that Laira worked this turn (one of the long-standing exchange duties) with this locomotive for no more than a month before the Moguls returned, the change of loco being largely at the insistence of the civil engineers. This picture shows Kings Road station in its final post-war guise, with the end wall completely removed. PHOTOGRAPH: ALAN LATHEY

former PD&SWJR 0-6-2Ts (Nos 30757 and 30758) spending lengthy periods in store at Friary, with only relatively brief outings on local shunting or relief work until their eventual transfer and subsequent demise. In 1953, the Ivatt tanks appeared at Barnstaple, and one consequence was that 'E1R' 0-6-2T No 32095

was transferred from there to Friary, where it joined No 32094. The latter engine was withdrawn in April 1955, but No 32096 took its place at Friary at the end of June.

On 28 November 1953 4056 of Bristol Bath Road was noted on Laira shed, where a 'Star' had become very much a

rarity. As a result of a breakaway on Dainton Bank on 22nd November Western Region traffic to and from Plymouth was routed over the Southern line - the largest WR types permitted were 2-6-0s, the up 'Cornish Riviera' being hauled from Plymouth by No.6319 'in solitary command of nine bogies'. All this was the very

Devonport Tunnel South, 18 March 1951. As explained earlier, SR/GWR exchange workings on passenger trains between Plymouth and Exeter were a regular occurrence for over twenty years. However, GWR goods workings on the SR route (and vice versa) were more usually a result of diversions, and so the sight of a WR-hauled down goods emerging from Devonport Tunnel (the grandiose term for the bridge on the SR line) was something unusual. Also noteworthy is the form of motive power, No.5976 ASHWICKE HALL. Although the 'Halls' performed reasonably regularly on the normal exchange duties in 1949-51, they were eventually prohibited from the SR line after accusations that they had re-profiled the platform faces at some intermediate stations. Due to this incompatibility, 'Halls' versus SR stations, the engines were, during their relatively brief period of use on the exchange workings, subjected to speed restrictions, but as the trains were stoppers the restriction wasn't at all troublesome. PHOTOGRAPH: ALAN LATHEY

Mutley, 15 December 1951. At the end of November, Exmouth Junction's short-stay Fairburn 2-6-4Ts had commenced a brief incumbency on workings between Exeter Central and Friary. Here, No.42105 - seemingly with a 75E (Three Bridges) shed plate - passes the site of Mutley station with the 11.35am Friary - Waterloo. **PHOTOGRAPH: ALAN LATHEY**

stuff of daily life in the 1950s, but mouth-wateringly nostalgic now. A stranger noted at Plymouth on 13th December 1953 was Tyseley 2-8-0 No.2856, which departed for Cornwall with a 16-coach empty stock train from Millbay. A rumour (unfounded) animated the locals, that 'Dukedog' 4-4-0s were to replace the 'Manor' 4-6-0s at Laira. Bristol standard '5MT' 4-6-0s became regular sights in Devon, Laira housing Nos.73028, 73032, 73033 and 73039 on 19th April 1954. 6018 KING HENRY VI was observed on the four coach 5.15pm Exeter - Plymouth local on 10th April and on 24th July all four Laira 'Britannia' Pacifics were out of service, No.70019 with a blown cylinder head. This presumably accounted for the appearance of Cardiff Canton Pacific No.70025 on the 4.20pm Plymouth - Kensington milk empties on 2nd August 1954.

Near Friary Junction, 10 August 1951. Mogul No.6397, still displaying its pre-Nationalisation ownership on the tender, canters up the slope from Friary Junction with the 11.47am local from Exeter Central. In the distance, the southern slopes of Dartmoor are visible. **PHOTOGRAPH: ALAN LATHEY**

Left:- Mount Gould Junction, 18 July 1951. The Laira - Friary transfer goods is hauled by 2-6-2T No.4518. The 4ft 6in gauge track of the Lee Moor Tramway is immediately behind the engine, the lines diverging to the right form the start of the Yealmpton branch, while the fork of the Lipson Junction and Laira Junction lines is visible in the distance. Allotments in the foreground, and reclaimed land on the right. PHOTOGRAPH: ALAN LATHEY

Right:- Sutton Harbour branch, 10 August 1951. Just six months before its withdrawal, '2021' class 0-6-0PT No.2148 - the regular branch engine at the time - hauls a train of empties towards the coal wharf at Sutton Harbour. The branch was double track throughout (except for the wharf sidings) until November 1936, when the northern section (seen here) was singled. The rest of the branch was singled in 1958. This picture was taken from Embankment Road, the lattice girder bridge in the background carrying the SR's Turnchapel branch - left for Friary, right for Turnchapel. The almost overgrown tracks on the embankment on the right are those of the Lee Moor Tramway, the section of the tramway south of Maddock's Concrete Works having fallen into disuse in 1947. Behind the photographer, the WR Sutton Harbour Branch veers westward (to the left) while the tramway continued in a south-easterly direction (to the right) to Laira Wharves at Cattedown. PHOTOGRAPH: ALAN LATHEY

Left:- Bull Point branch, 10 April 1952. Providing another foray into Plymouth's lesser-known railway by-ways, 0-6-0PT No.4693 returns from Bull Point to St.Budeaux with the branch transfer freight. Bull Point siding opened in July 1916 to serve the Admiralty's armaments depot. The depot had an internal 1ft 6in gauge tramway which was initially worked by diminutive Wingrove & Rogers battery electric locomotives and, later, equally small Ruston & Hornsby diesels. The locomotives were replaced by road tractors in 1958. PHOTOGRAPH: ALAN LATHEY

Near Laira Bridge, 2 April 1952. The Cattewater branch goods, returning to Friary, passes under Laira Bridge Road; part of Laira Bridge itself can just be seen on the extreme left of the picture. 'B4' No.30094 is in charge. The primitive track on the right is that of the horse-worked 4ft 6in gauge Lee Moor Tramway, this section having fallen into disuse in 1947. Readers familiar with the sartorial aspect of railway staffing might wish to look closely at the outfit worn by the man standing alongside the engine - is it a full SR goods guard's uniform? PHOTOGRAPH: ALAN LATHEY

Right:- Cattewater branch, 1 June 1953. The Esso depot at Cattewater was located in a former quarry (the intriguingly named Deadman's Bay Quarry), rail access being by means of a spur which passed through a hole in the rock face. 'B4' No.30089 emerges from the 'tunnel' prior to joining the branch proper. PHOTOGRAPH: ALAN LATHEY

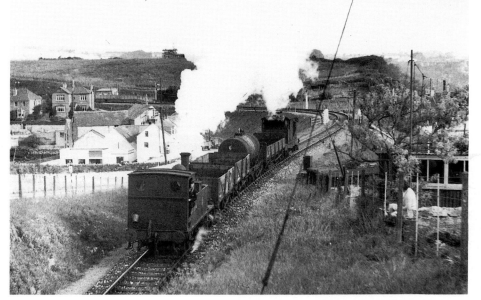

Left:- The morning goods to Turnchapel is hauled by 'B4' 0-4-0T No.30094 near Plymstock, 15 September 1955. Plymstock station - where the Turnchapel branch diverged from the GWR's Yealmpton branch - is just discernible in the background (above the engine's cab). Oreston Road is alongside the railway, on the left. This could be a rural branch line almost anywhere in Britain, but the centre of a major city is less than two miles away. Indeed, since 1967 the area seen here has actually been incorporated in the City of Plymouth itself. PHOTOGRAPH: ALAN LATHEY

Approaching Friary Junction, 4 March 1954. Lightweight Pacific No.34013 OKEHAMPTON hauls the through train for Brighton, the locomotive working as far as Salisbury. The platform on the right - from which the picture was taken - is that of Lucas Terrace Halt; closed in 1951, it once served Turnchapel branch trains.
PHOTOGRAPH: ALAN LATHEY

Mutley, 8 July 1961. An interesting cross section - SR Mogul No.31903 on an empty stock working, a 'Type 2' diesel-hydraulic, 'Castle' No.7022.
PHOTOGRAPH R C RILEY.

Near Lipson Junction, 4 July 1957. Much has been said about the use of GWR/WR engines on SR services between Friary and Plymouth, and here are two examples together. The 11.47am Exeter Central - Friary train (nearest the camera) is hauled by No.6385, the 2.25pm from Friary being entrusted to fellow Mogul No.5376.
PHOTOGRAPH: R.C. RILEY

Near Laira Junction, 16 July 1956. 2-6-2T No.4592 approaches the junction with a two-coach non-corridor 'B' set from Launceston. The tracks immediately behind the engine were laid as dead-end sidings in 1936; the nearer of the two was lengthened and converted to a through track in 1943, while the farther one - Ocean Siding - retained its dead-end status. PHOTOGRAPH: ALAN LATHEY

Lipsom Vale, 24 August 1952. '57XX' class 0-6-0PT No.7762 heads west with with a train of ballast hoppers. The allotments on the right were on railway land - a reminder of the 'dig for victory' campaign of the war years. Another reminder of the war is provided by the Anderson shelter. PHOTOGRAPH: ALAN LATHEY

Devonport (Kings Road) station, probably 1956. 'O2' 0-4-4T No.30183 was a fairly long-standing Plymouth resident, working the St.Budeaux and Tavistock locals, piloting at Kings Road and, occasionally, deputising for Ivatt 2-6-2Ts on the Callington branch services until the early 1960s. It is seen here at Kings Road station which seemed to enjoy something of the air of tranquillity and spaciousness more typical of a rural outpost. These days, a visit to the still-operational Exeter Central station can provide an uncanny likeness to how things used to be at Kings Road. PHOTOGRAPH: R.C. RILEY COLLECTION

Stanier 2-8-0s Nos.48420 and 48472 were loaned to the WR and both were at Plymouth in early August; Laira lost its five 'Manors', 7804, 7809, 7814, 7815 and 7824, to standard '4MT' Moguls Nos.75025-75029.

On 7th October 1954 an Ocean Liner Express was worked from Plymouth Docks to Paddington in 3hr 37min (5069 ISAMBARD KINGDOM BRUNEL with a five-coach 171ton loading); on 22nd 5058 EARL OF CLANCARTY managed the same timing, but with a seven coach 226ton train. One of Exmouth Junctions standard '3MT' 2-6-2Ts, No.82022, was reported working to Plymouth via Newton Abbot; on 15th and 16th December 1954 it headed the 11.25am from St.Davids and the 4.32pm back from Plymouth....

During the following year - 1955 - local activities included an LM Pacific No. 46237 on loan to the WR for road tests, making its first trip to Plymouth on 10th May. Shrewsbury 'County' No.1025 appeared in Plymouth with a Manchester relief on 21st and Bournemouth Pacific No.34044 headed the 11.15am ex-Waterloo into Plymouth on 23rd. That same month, 4-4-0 No.9023 arrived with a fish

Devonport (Kings Road) station, undated. Exmouth Junction's No.34069 HAWKINGE pulls out of Kings Road with a train for Exeter or beyond. PHOTOGRAPH: R.C. RILEY

its impending arrival had to be hastily wired through to Laira. Because of a diversion, 'Castles' worked over the SR route to/from Plymouth for the first time on 11th November, No.5057 being on the 1.40am Crewe - Plymouth and the 5.5pm perishable from Millbay, No.7031 on the 1.30pm Paddington - Plymouth and the 4.45pm ex-Penzance, No.4087 on the up 'Riviera', No.5098 on the 1.20pm ex-Penzance, and No.4077 on the 12.35pm ex-Penzance.

Laira acquired Exeter's two 'Castles', 5003 and 5021 early in 1957 whilst the newly named 'Mayflower' got off to a dubious start, the timetables being disrupted by three boat specials from Plymouth, and the inaugural train carrying Princess Margaret (hauled by 6028 KING GEORGE VI) was therefore divided to enable Her Royal Highness to leave on time. On August 31 the boat train portion for *Reina Del Mar* passengers was attached at Plymouth to the 8.20am Plymouth - Paddington, and the heavy 15-coach loading (including a 41-ton kitchen car) was double-headed throughout by 5021 WHITTINGTON CASTLE and 6000 KING GEORGE V. On 12 September 1957 4-4-0 CITY OF TRURO arrived at Laira, having come down from Swindon as a pilot on the 5.30am Paddington - Penzance; the veteran 4-4-0 was to be used on a Plymouth - Penzance excursion on 15 September.

In 1958, correspondents noted a few tastes of things to come: 0-6-0 diesel shunters Nos.11225-11229 (later Nos D2225-2229) arrived for work on the Turnchapel and Cattewater lines, and as a result the Plymouth Friary 'B4' 0-4-0Ts were thrown out of work. An indirect outcome of the transfer of territory between the WR and the SR on February 1, was that the four Bulleid Pacifics at Friary,

Cornwall Junction, 17 July 1956. Looking in quite good cosmetic condition, 0-4-2T No.1434 rounds the curve at Cornwall Junction en route to North Road with empty stock (viz., one trailer car) from Millbay. PHOTOGRAPH: R.C. RILEY

train from Swindon, while 14XX 0-4-2Ts Nos.1408 and 1438 appeared, for auto train duties on the Tavistock branch.

By 1956, there were new standard '4MT' 4-6-0s at Exmouth Junction, and they were engaged principally on the Okehampton - Plymouth workings. On-loan Stanier Pacific No.46210 headed the 'Cornish Riviera' into Plymouth on 10th February, but its brick arch collapsed and it had to join the 'Kings' it was intended to replace (Nos. 6000, 6004, 6017, 6022 and 6027) stored at Laira minus their front bogies. The winter diagrams (1956/ 57) included three day trips to London and back for Laira double-chimney 'Kings' - the 7.15am Plymouth - Paddington and 6.30pm back, the 12.30pm Plymouth - Paddington and the 9.50pm back, and the 2pm Plymouth - Paddington and the 12.30am newspapers back. On 6th October 1956 Stafford Road King No.6011 worked the 3.30pm Paddington - Plymouth, and as the engine was fitted with experimental water-softening apparatus,

Kings Road, early 1960s. The rebuilt Pacifics were initially prohibited from the Exeter - Plymouth line due to their increased weight, but the ban was lifted in 1960 and by the following year the rebuilt engines were in charge of most of the regular Exeter - Plymouth passenger workings. The engine here, No.34104 BERE ALSTON, was not rebuilt until May 1961, and Kings Road station was closed to passenger traffic in September 1964, and so that narrows down the date of the picture somewhat. PHOTOGRAPH: R.C. RILEY COLLECTION

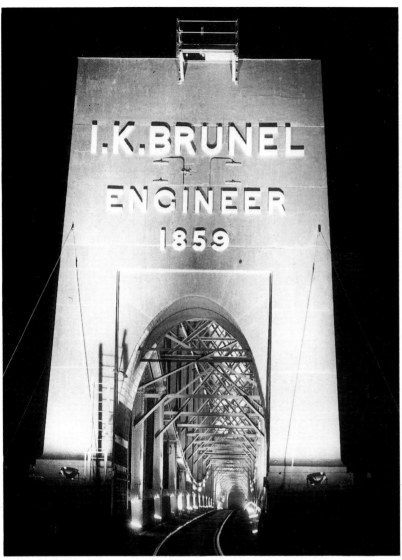

1 May 1959. The centenary of the opening of the Royal Albert Bridge and the Cornwall Railway was commemorated by the floodlighting of the bridge portals - but why didn't the official photographer arrange for the ladder on the left to be straightened or, better still, dispensed with it altogether? Another event to mark the centenary was the unveiling of a plaque in Brunel's memory at Saltash station.

Nos.34035-34038, moved to Exmouth Junction (Friary shed was transferred to the WR on 23 February 1958 and was recoded 83H). The prototype 'Warship' diesel-hydraulic D600 ACTIVE made its first visit to its eventual home on March 19, when it worked a 10-coach test train from Swindon to Plymouth, reaching 'home' fifteen minutes early. In July both the North British 2,000hp diesel-hydraulic units so far placed in service, D600 and D601, were working between Plymouth and Penzance and on July 19 D601 ARK ROYAL, piloted by a St.Blazey 'Manor', 7816, worked the 10.35am ex-Paddington from Plymouth. The new Swindon-built D800 worked the down 'Cornish Riviera' to Plymouth on July 15; at Plymouth D601 was due to take over, but it failed completely leaving Laira and 6907 DAVENHAM HALL had to be hurriedly substituted. For the first time a rebuilt 'Merchant Navy', No.35023, reached Plymouth, on September 20. It travelled down on the 11.25am stopping train from Exeter in order to take over at Plymouth the 'West Countryman' excursion. The two 'T9' 4-4-0s, Nos.30712 and 30726, which the Pacific replaced at North Road, followed up on the 4.32pm stopping train to Exeter. D800 worked the 5.40pm parcels from Swindon to Plymouth on September 12 as a prelude to working from Laira.

Despite the transfer of Friary shed to the WR in February 1958, its allocation remained largely Southern-oriented. At the time of the transfer Friary had four 'O2' 0-4-4Ts, and these were taken into WR stock, remaining at work on local services, sometimes deputising for the Ivatt 2-6-2Ts on the Callington branch and occasionally piloting at King's Road, Devonport. Three were retired in April 1962, the fourth having been returned to

Left:- Royal Albert Bridge, 3 October 1959. One of the less well-photographed members of its class, No.4950 PATSHULL HALL, clears the single line section of the bridge and the fireman prepares to hand over the tablet. The working is an up milk train, possibly the 12.25pm Penzance - Kensington and the apparently light loading wasn't such an easy task for the engine as might be thought - on curves, a loaded six-wheeled milk wagon with bad friction on the middle axle was, in effect, the equivalent of a fully-loaded bogie carriage. Hence the usual use of big engines on milk trains, often the enigmatic 47XX 2-8-0s, eastwards from Plymouth. The 47XXs were, incidentally, prohibited from crossing the Royal Albert Bridge, the only other GWR type similarly banned being the 'Kings', although the latter type did venture into Cornwall on at least two occasions. The bridge was treated to major refurbishment in 1967-69, and this enabled it to accommodate the 25-ton axleweights of BR's new 100-ton bogie tank wagons. The speed limit on the bridge was 15mph, but in practice that wasn't always observed. PHOTOGRAPH: TERRY NICHOLLS

North Road station, 1959. The German-influenced D800 series of diesel-hydraulics - introduced in August 1958 and seventy-one strong by June 1962 - were, arguably, as successful as the D600s were unsuccessful. The D800s were used on Paddington - Plymouth workings from the outset, and the early class members were all allocated to Laira from new. D801 VANGUARD brings the down 'Riviera' into North Road. PHOTOGRAPH: MICHAEL MENSING

SR stock earlier that year. Furthermore, two of Friary's 'M7s', 30034 and 30036, remained reasonably active at Friary (under WR auspices) almost until the end of steam workings in the Plymouth area.

Another long-term change in hand at that time was the rebuilding of the light-weight Bulleid Pacifics. The programme commenced in 1957, and as the work increased the engines' axle-weights from 18tons 15cwt to 20tons 18cwt, the rebuilt engines were barred from the North Devon, Cornwall and Plymouth lines. In 1960, however, the prohibition over the Plymouth line was lifted and, by 1961, most of the Plymouth - Exeter passenger workings were being handled by the rebuilt Pacifics, though their re-emergence was to be rather brief.

Returning to the reports of the *Trains Illustrated* observers, in 1959 they noted that five main line diesel-hydraulics, D800 and D801 and D600 - D602, were officially allocated to Laira at the start of

Right:- Devonport (Kings Road) station, 1 August 1964. The 'Warship' diesels were soon augmented and, to a great extent, eventually displaced by the more-powerful 'Westerns' (Class '52s'). The 'Warships' were then often seen on secondary routes including, for a short while, the old SR line between Plymouth and Exeter. Just over a month before the withdrawal of passenger services from that route, D824 HIGHFLYER brings the 11.30 Brighton - Plymouth train into Kings Road; since the closure to passenger traffic of the SR station at Friary in 1958, the service had inevitably terminated at North Road. One item of interest - the doorways behind the platform on the right are those of the long since disused engine shed at Devonport. PHOTOGRAPH: S.C. NASH

Right:- Royal Albert Bridge, 25 April 1958. The irreversible change in the face of WR motive power started in 1958, the prototype 'Warship' diesel-hydraulics, D600 ACTIVE and D601 ARK ROYAL, being introduced early that year. During that summer they were the only two examples, D602/603 not appearing until November 1958 and D604 in January 1959. During part of that first summer (1958) D600 and D601 worked between Plymouth and Penzance, but by the autumn they were diagrammed to work between Plymouth and Paddington. At the outset much was expected of the new machines, hence the welter of official publicity pictures of high-profile workings - in this instance D600 approaching Saltash with the down 'Riviera'. This belied their disastrous availability figures and they remained humiliatingly unique - an entire main line class doomed to stay 'close to home' rather than risk a longer journey...

Laira, 30 August 1961. Almost-new D853 THRUSTER, one of the North British 'Warships', has the equally new WR chocolate and cream dynamometer car, DW150192, attached prior to trials. The car had been converted from a Hawksworth third, No.796 of 1946, to replace the Churchward vehicle of 1901, and was principally intended for the testing of new diesels. At the more traditional end of the scale, the locomotive used for shunting the dynamometer car is 0-6-0ST No.1363, which spent almost all of its fifty-odd year life in the Plymouth area. PHOTOGRAPH: R.C. RILEY

the year; moreover Type 2s D6301 and D6302 were working from Swindon to Plymouth by March. A 2-10-0 was recorded at Plymouth for the first time on February 21, No.92235 working the 2.30pm Hackney (Newton Abbot) - Tavistock Junction, and Laira very soon acquired 2-10-0s of its own, Nos 92208 and 92221-92225. Other 2-10-0s were used on Saturday trains to and from Plymouth, 92205 hauling the 7.35am Plymouth - Paddington for instance on July 4, 92249 the 1.20pm Plymouth - Paddington on July 25, 92206 the up 'Mayflower' on August 8, while 92222 was in charge of the 10.5am Penzance - Manchester (which was booked as a through engine working from Plymouth to Shrewsbury) on August 8.

From then on, the everyday reports of locomotive activities were not for the faint-hearted steam enthusiast. However, the original 'Warships', Nos D600-604, proved spectacularly unreliable and spent much of their lives at Laira, from where they could be kept out of harm's way on the Plymouth - Penzance section. They were mercifully done away with at the end of 1967. The later 'Warships', D800-D870, proved far superior, and became a regular feature on the main line passenger workings to and from Plymouth. As early as April 1960, *The Railway Magazine* reported that the dozen or so delivered by then were all based at Laira, and nor-

mally worked 'nearly all the trains between Paddington and the West of England, including the night postal trains, and other services routed via Bristol'. It was also noted that a recent allocation list showed only three 'Kings' on the Laira books - the shed had once been a strong-hold of the class.

The 'Warships' were later permitted on the Exeter - Okehampton - Plymouth route in cases of emergency, and such an instance occurred in December 1960 when floods caused immense disruption in the Exeter area. The 'Warship' complement

Laira Junction, 30 August 1961. The North British Type '2' diesel-hydraulics, introduced in January 1959, had similar route availability to '45XX' 2-6-2Ts but, of course, with far more power. With such a highly useful combination of attributes they were used extensively in Devon and Cornwall, performing, within the constraints of their reliability, a wide variety of duties. Assisting heavy trains over the South Devon banks was just one task - this is D6334 piloting No.5090 NEATH ABBEY. PHOTOGRAPH: R.C. RILEY

North Road Station - arrivals and departures of Western Region services
(i.e. excluding trains to and from Friary station), summer Saturdays 1955.

2.45am ex-Newcastle to Penzance dep. 2.50am *
3.05am ex-Paddington to Penzance dep. 3.10pm *
3.25am ex-Newcastle to Newquay dep. 3.30am *
3.40am ex-Paddington to Penzance dep. 3.45am
3.50am ex-Paddington to Newquay dep. 4.00am *
4.40am ex-Paddington to Penzance dep. 4.50am
4.55am ex-Wolverhampton to Penzance dep. 5.00am *
5.30am to Saltash
5.35am ex-Paddington
5.50am to Tavistock South
6.00am ex-Paddington to Penzance dep. 6.05am *
6.10am to Liskeard
6.20am ex-Manchester to Newquay dep. 6.25am *
6.30am to Saltash
6.31pm ex-Saltash
6.43am to Saltash
6.47am ex-St.Austell
6.50am to Penzance
7.00am to Paddington
7.10am to Launceston
7.11am ex-Saltash
7.24am to St.Germans
7.25am to Paddington *
7.30am ex-Tavistock South
7.34am ex-Saltash
7.35am ex-Paddington to Penzance dep. 7.45am
7.45am to Tavistock South
7.50am ex-Glasgow *
8.08am ex-Plympton to Saltash dep. 8.10am
8.11am ex-Liskeard
8.20am ex-Manchester to Penzance dep. 8.30am *
8.30am to Paddington
8.32am ex-St.Germans
8.38am to Saltash
8.45am to Liverpool
8.47am ex-Saltash
8.47am ex-Launceston
8.48am ex-Newton Abbot
8.54am to Saltash
9.00am ex-St.Austell to Birmingham dep. 9.10am
9.10am to Penzance
9.16am ex-Saltash
9.20am ex-Truro to Newton Abbot dep. 9.30am
9.26am ex-Tavistock South
9.40am to St.Germans
9.42am ex-Saltash
9.43am ex-Newton Abbot
9.55am ex-Newquay to Manchester dep. 10.05am
10.10am ex-Newquay to Newcastle dep. 10.18am *
10.20am to Menheniot
10.20am ex-Saltash
10.25am to Launceston
10.25am ex-Penzance to Wolverhampton dep. 10.30am
10.30am ex-Liverpool to Penzance dep. 10.40am
10.43am to Penzance
10.45am ex-Manchester
11.05am ex-St.Germans
11.15am to Paddington
11.15am to Saltash
11.20am ex-Penzance to Paddington dep. 11.30am
11.30am ex-Paddington to Penzance dep. 11.40am

11.38am ex-Truro
11.50am ex-St.Ives to Paddington dep. 12.00
11.50am ex-Swindon to Penzance dep. 12.00
11.55am ex-Launceston to Redruth dep. 12.05pm
12.08pm to Launceston
12.20pm ex-Penzance to Paddington dep. 12.30pm ¶
12.30pm to Saltash
12.35pm to Newton Abbot
12.40pm ex-Menheniot
12.45pm to Tavistock South
12.45pm ex-Bristol to Penzance dep. 12.50pm *
12.50pm ex-Penzance
12.55pm ex-Birmingham to Penzance dep. 1.00pm *
1.00pm ex-Newquay to York dep. 1.10pm
1.05pm to Saltash
1.10pm ex-Penzance to Cardiff dep. 1.25pm
1.10pm ex-Ealing Broadway to Penzance dep. 1.20pm
1.20pm ex-Tavistock South
1.22pm ex-Saltash
1.30pm to St.Germans
1.30pm ex-Newquay to Wolverhampton dep. 1.35pm *
1.35pm ex-Paddington to Penzance dep. 1.40pm *
1.40pm ex-Penzance to Sheffield dep. 1.50pm
1.51pm ex-Saltash
1.52pm to Saltash
1.56pm ex-Newton Abbot
2.00pm ex-Penzance to Wolverhampton dep. 2.05pm
2.10pm to Tavistock South
2.10pm to Truro
2.15pm ex-Newquay to Paddington. dep. 2.20pm
2.20pm ex-Paddington to Newquay dep. 2.24pm
2.28pm ex-Launceston
2.29pm ex-Saltash
2.30pm to Exeter
2.35pm to Saltash
2.40pm ex-Penzance to Paddington dep. 2.50pm
2.55pm ex-St.Germans
3.00pm to Saltash
3.10pm to Launceston
3.10pm ex-Paddington to Penzance dep. 3.15pm
3.15pm ex-Saltash
3.30pm ex-Wolverhampton to Penzance dep. 3.35pm
3.30pm ex-Penzance to Glasgow dep. 3.45pm
3.45pm ex-Paddington to Penzance dep. 3.55pm
3.47pm ex-Newquay to Paddington dep. 3.55pm *
3.50pm ex-Launceston
4.00pm ex-Penzance to Paddington dep. 4.10pm
4.10pm to Saltash
4.20pm ex-Paddington to Penzance dep. 4.25pm
4.26pm ex-Saltash
4.32pm to Exeter
4.35pm to Saltash
4.37pm ex-Nottingham
4.45pm ex-Carmarthen to Penzance dep. 4.55pm *
5.02pm ex-Saltash
5.05pm ex-Bristol to Penzance dep. 5.14pm
5.09pm to Saltash
5.17pm ex-Tavistock South
5.18pm ex-Penzance to Newton Abbot dep. 5.40pm
5.25pm to Tavistock South
5.27pm ex-Saltash
5.35pm to Liskeard

5.38pm ex-Paddington
5.50pm to Saltash
5.55pm ex-Manchester to Penzance dep. 6.00pm
6.02pm ex-Saltash
6.07pm to Bristol
6.15pm to Saltash
6.20pm ex-Liverpool to Penzance dep. 6.28pm
6.23pm to Launceston
6.30pm ex-Birkenhead
6.30pm ex-Saltash
6.40pm ex-Exeter
6.44pm to St.Germans
6.52pm ex-Saltash
6.55pm ex-Paddington to Penzance dep. 7.04pm
7.02pm ex-Penzance to Newton Abbot dep. 7.10pm
7.24pm ex-Liskeard
7.25pm ex-Launceston
7.30pm ex-Liverpool
7.38pm to Saltash
7.47pm ex-Saltash
7.50pm ex-Tavistock South
7.56pm to Saltash
7.58pm ex-Penzance to Manchester dep. 8.05pm
8.00pm ex-Paddington to Penzance dep. 8.07pm
8.15pm ex-Newquay *
8.24pm to Launceston
8.25pm to Doublebois
8.50pm ex-Saltash
9.00pm to Saltash
9.02pm ex-Newton Abbot
9.20pm to Saltash
9.45pm ex-Manchester
9.56pm ex-Saltash
10.00pm ex-Paddington
10.00pm ex-Launceston
10.15pm ex-Penzance to Manchester dep. 10.25pm *
10.25pm to Saltash
10.40pm ex-Penzance
11.03pm ex-Saltash
11.12pm ex-Paddington
11.15pm to Doublebois
11.20pm ex-Penzance to Paddington dep. 11.45pm
11.40pm ex-Penzance to Paddington dep. 12.00
12.40am ex-Paddington
12.40am ex-Penzance to Paddington dep. 1.00am
* did not operate at given time for whole duration of summer timetable
¶ 'Cornish Riviera Express'
In addition to the numerous services listed above, there were also four trains which were intended to pass through Plymouth non-stop. Their approximate passing times were:
 10.50am Perranporth-Paddington
 11.00am Falmouth-Paddington
 12.10pm Newquay-Paddington
 3.05pm Paddington-Penzance ('Cornish Riviera')
Under normal circumstances, the down 'Riviera' definitely passed through without stopping, its engine having been changed at Newton Abbot. The three non-stop Paddington services would have changed engines somewhere *en route*, but it is unknown to this writer whether the change was made at North Road, Laira or Newton Abbot. Polite enlightenment positively welcomed!

Approaching Laira Junction, 7 July 1963. The new order not only cometh - here it outnumbereth. A down express, double-headed by North British Type '2' D6332 and 'Warship' D827, pass an engineer's train, hauled by the now-preserved No.4555. PHOTOGRAPH: R.C. RILEY

fer were four 2-6-2Ts, 41302, 41315, 41316 and 41317, which retained their duties on the Callington branch until the dieselisation of that line in 1964. Laira did not have long as a steam shed, either. As early as 1957 two roads of the straight shed had been screened off for diesels, and by 1959 plans were in hand to rebuild this 'long shed' entirely for diesel maintenance - in the event, as the new glass and concrete depot arose alongside, the straight shed in fact *reverted* to steam for a short while. A 12,000-gallon diesel oil tank was nevertheless installed alongside one of the

Left:- Laira, 2 May 1959. Although this picture was taken principally to show 0-6-0PT No.6420 with the four-coach RCTS 'Plymouth District Rail Tour' (seen here en route from Millbay to Friary), the presence of two 'D600' diesels at Laira depot - one outside the straight shed and one on the chord line behind the train - demonstrate that the new era has dawned. **PHOTOGRAPH: P.W. GRAY**

at Laira was eventually boosted by examples displaced elsewhere by the more-powerful 'Westerns' (introduced in 1961), and a few later found their way to Laira. The North British 'D63XXs' were always very well represented at Laira, although the Western Region's other early main line diesels, the 'Hymeks', took a little while to gravitate there. In later years, LMR 'Peak' Type 4s frequently worked through to Plymouth, and in due course Nos 46001-46011 were based at Laira.

At the start of 1963 everything west of Wilton (near Salisbury) passed to the WR, and partly due to the Region's enthusiasm for eliminating steam west of Exeter, Friary shed closed in May. Its remaining engines were transferred to Laira (which was recoded 84A in September 1963, its last sub-shed - at Launceston - having closed at the end of 1962), but it appears that the only locomotives which survived long enough to be involved in the trans-

Above:- Laira, 27 January 1962. The diesels in the straight shed (in the mid-distance on the left) are very evident. Not too far away at Home Park, Plymouth Argyle are playing the mighty Tottenham Hotspur - Jimmy Greaves, Alan Gilzean, Dave Mackay and all - in the F.A.Cup. It has been suggested that No.1001 COUNTY OF BUCKS worked a supporters' special up from Penzance, but as 1001 was a Didcot engine at the time it might have actually brought Spurs fans from London. Whatever the case, local engine No.4087 CARDIGAN CASTLE had, apparently, piloted another 'Castle' (possibly No.5015) on the 5.45am Broxbourne - Plymouth and returned as pilot to No.7022 with the 6.20pm Plymouth - Broxbourne. **PHOTOGRAPH: P.W. GRAY**

Left:- Laira, 1960/61. Hardly a wisp of smoke anywhere - despite the not-insignificant contingent of steam engines on shed. The new diesel depot is under construction (on the left, partly out of frame) on the site of the recently-removed up sidings.

heavy oil tanks which had been provided in the late 1940s, and the two water columns were removed, and the mains blanked off.

Within a few years a brand new diesel depot was constructed near the steam shed. The old steam shed was then quietly done away with. Laira diesel depot - the Western Region's first - opened in the autumn of 1961. In the July 1964 issue of *Modern Railways*, G.Freeman Allen explained that '...dieselisation of the Plymouth Division is near totality', revealing that only two steam locos were still based on ex-GWR depots west of Exeter. Both of them were at Laira and would have gone even before the report went to press. Some facilities had to be retained at Laira, for many steam locos were still sent into the Plymouth Division - much more, Freeman Allan recorded, than the local authorities cared for. As many as eight steam locomotives had turned up in one day - such numbers could cause 'fair havoc, with rosters framed exclusively for diesels that are capable of a quick turnround'.

By the time that piece was published,

Top:- Laira, 23 July 1963. The new diesel depot from the south. The DMU in the foreground is over the bogie washing pit, which was later covered by a lightweight shelter. Bogie washing presented a problem - if neglected, the build-up of grease and oil presented a very real fire hazard but, if performed too zealously or regularly, rubber seals could dry out and perish. A bit like steam cleaning your car's engine, in fact. The tall building running lengthwise through the depot is the maintenance hall - locomotive access from the north end only. The old steam shed can be seen on the left of the frame, behind the 'mullet pond'.

Middle:- Laira, 28 June 1962. The Lee Moor Tramway was officially closed in October 1960; the old down yard at Laira, with which the tramway enjoyed interchange facilities, was converted to carriage sidings, brought into use early in 1961. In case this viewpoint of the defunct LMT seems unfamiliar, we are looking south-west, the bridge carrying Embankment Road over the main Plymouth - Exeter line being on the left. The disused tramway is clearly visible leading away from the foreground, Laira Junction Signalbox is in the mid-distance, and the roof of the diesel depot maintenance hall lies in the distance on the right.

Right:- Laira, 28 June 1962. Another entertainingly different view of the course of the disused Lee Moor Tramway. The bridge on the right of the picture carries Embankment Road over the tramway - Lower Crabtree is beyond, and Laira behind. The roundabout connecting Embankment Road, Old Laira Road and Plymouth Road is virtually where the motor-bike and sidecar are parked at the top of the slope, the roundabout being considerably enlarged in the 1970s. The Ford Thames van - air-controlled windscreen wipers and double-jointed gear linkage. Once experienced, never forgotten!

Laira, 27 August 1961. As part of the overall improvements in the Plymouth area in the late 1950s and early 1960s, much-needed carriage sidings replaced the old down sidings on the east side of the Laira Junction - Mount Gould Junction line. 'O2' 0-4-4T No.30225 became the last of its class at Plymouth; on its retirement at the end of 1962, withdrawn classmate No.30200 was earmarked to take its place, but the latter didn't actually leave the scrap sidings at Eastleigh. PHOTOGRAPH: R.C. RILEY (COLLECTION)

describer apparatus, and it controls an area from Lipson Junction to Keyham.

The rebuilding of North Road station is making considerable progress, and the new 10-storey administrative block has begun to climb above the surrounding buildings.

The 'new' North Road station comprised seven platform faces and a pair of small loading docks at the east end of the down side. The loading docks were on the site of what had, in 1938, been designated Platform One (a bay for Tavistock branch trains), but a new parcels depot was built on the site instead and the designation 'Platform One' was subsequently abandoned. Consequently, the seven platforms (all of which serviced through roads) were designated 2 to 8, numbered south to north.

The new parcels depot at North Road replaced the former depot at the west end of the station. The old depot had been closed in September 1957, temporary facilities having been provided at Devonport (Kings Road) station until the completion of new premises at North Road. The new

Laira had indeed been officially closed to steam - for some three months - and on 7 September 1964, steam was effectively eliminated west of Exeter.

One of the biggest changes at Plymouth during the 1960s was the completion of the rebuilding of North Road station, work having recommenced in 1956. Extensive resignalling was also undertaken, a press release of November 1960 proclaiming that: *Plymouth's new master signal box, sited at the west end of North Road station, took over the functions of six existing cabins (Lipson Junction, Plymouth North Road East and West, Cornwall Junction, Devonport Junction and Devonport Albert Road) when the Plymouth colour-light resignalling scheme was completed on 26 November 1960. It was the first fully-operational box on the WR to employ the new four-character train*

Above:- Laira Junction, 30 August 1961. The delightful little '1361' class 0-6-0STs have been under-represented in this book, maybe, but this splendid picture goes part of the way to redress the balance. It's No.1363 - a Plymouth engine for most of its life - passing the junction signalbox with a transfer goods from Laira shed to Tavistock Junction. Note the shunting arm (in the lower left-hand corner) for controlling horse-drawn Lee Moor traffic. At the opposite end of the signalling scale, the new colour light signals on the down main line can be seen. PHOTOGRAPH: R.C. RILEY

Left:- Laira Junction, 30 September 1961. A train of china clay wagons, presumably from ECC's dryers at Marsh Mills, heads west, possibly for export via Fowey or St.Austell. Since 1960, china clay had been brought down in liquid form to Marsh Mills by means of the newly-installed pipeline. The locomotive is No.6873 CARADOC GRANGE. PHOTOGRAPH: R.C. RILEY

Left:- Laira Junction, 1 December 1962. The Tavistock auto, hauled by 0-6-0PT No.6400, passes Laira Junction signalbox. Yet again, the Embankment Road bridge provides an excellent photographic viewpoint - there must have been times when the bridge parapets seemed like the venue for a camera club outing. The pile of rails on part of the carriage sidings (on the right) provides ample evidence of the immense changes underway in the immediate area.
PHOTOGRAPH: TERRY NICHOLLS

North Road signalbox, incidentally, was built on the site of the old parcels depot.

The new station was ceremonially opened on 26 March 1962 (24 years after rebuilding had officially commenced), the guest of honour on 'opening' day being one Dr. Richard Beeching.

The rebuilding of North Road station was part of a massive modernisation scheme in the Plymouth area. Another part of the works involved the laying of new sidings to the east of North Road station, partly on the site of the up platform of the then-deceased Mutley station, which had closed on 3 July 1939. Mutley had opened in August 1871 and had been jointly used by the GWR and LSWR, the latter having had its own staff there. It had become known as 'the gentry's station', due to its typically well-heeled clientele.

Another aspect of the modernisation work at Plymouth was the demolition of

Above:- North Road station, 12 July 1956. The rebuilding of the down side of the station is in hand, but more or less impossible to discern from this distance. An up stopping train, with No.6848 TODDINGTON GRANGE in charge, pulls out of Platform 8. **PHOTOGRAPH: R.C. RILEY**

Left:- North Road station, 18 July 1956. Looking west, the rebuilding work on the down side of the station is at last in hand. West signalbox (on the far side of the station) was superseded in 1960 by the new 'Plymouth' power box (on the left-hand side of the running lines). The 'Castle' in the distance appears to be shunting vans.
PHOTOGRAPH: R.C. RILEY

Above:- North Road station, 8 April 1960. With the rebuilding work still in progress, Penzance based No. 6826 NANNERTH GRANGE stands at Platform 3 with a ballast train. PHOTOGRAPH: R.C. RILEY

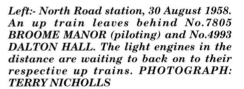

Left:- North Road station, 30 August 1958. An up train leaves behind No.7805 BROOME MANOR (piloting) and No.4993 DALTON HALL. The light engines in the distance are waiting to back on to their respective up trains. PHOTOGRAPH: TERRY NICHOLLS

Left:- North Road station, 8 August 1959. No.6860 ABERPORTH GRANGE is off the road at the east end of the station, and No.1006 COUNTY OF CORNWALL has been given the task of trying to tow its fellow Penzance engine back on to the rails. The attempt was unsuccessful and the timing couldn't really have been worse - it was a peak-summer Saturday. PHOTOGRAPH: TERRY NICHOLLS

the two island platforms at Millbay to make room for new carriage sidings. Carriage stabling had been a long-term problem in and around Plymouth as, unlike many other major rail centres, its main station (North Road) had minimal stabling facilities.

On the freight side, Tavistock Junction concentration yard (to the east of the city) was enlarged by 1958, and this enabled Laira Yard to be closed at the end of the year. Tavistock Junction did not, however, handle all of the freight traffic in the Plymouth area. On 15 September 1958, Friary station was closed to passenger traffic (empty SR coaching stock subsequently using part of the Laira Yard site), and was converted for use as Plymouth's main goods depot.

On 7 September 1964 the ex-PD&SWJR line south of St.Budeaux was closed, trains on the Okehampton route subsequently being diverted via the ex-GWR line at St.Budeaux by means of a 'temporary' connection which had been laid during the war. This brought about the closure of the former PD&SWJR/LSWR station at Devonport (and also Ford station) and, with Friary station having closed to passengers six years previously, North Road station was retitled, more simply, 'Plymouth'.

Following the closure of the old PD&SWJR line southwards from St.Budeaux in 1964, the revised route into Plymouth from Okehampton was, therefore, via Keyham. That, however, lasted only until 6 June 1968 when passenger services were withdrawn between

North Road East, 14 June 1959. Light engine movements between North Road and Laira were a long-standing problem, even more acute during the peak season, and only partly alleviated by the provision, as far back as 1913, of basic servicing facilities at Cornwall Junction. Engines are No.6863 DOLHYWEL GRANGE, No.6845 PAVILAND GRANGE, No.6025 KING HENRY III and No.7820 DINMORE MANOR. PHOTOGRAPH: TERRY NICHOLLS

Okehampton and Plymouth (apart from the locals to Gunnislake - the point at which the Callington branch had been truncated in November 1966). To LSWR/SR traditionalists it seemed that, after all that time, Paddington had finally got back at its old rival.

The foregoing is only a condensed account of the alterations at Plymouth during the 1960s. An excellent account of the modernisation work and the changes in

traffic operation in the Plymouth area was given in the July and August 1962 issues of *Modern Railways,* by R.C. Riley.

To end on a sombre note, there was yet another casualty during the 1960s. This involved the 'Atlantic Coast Express' - whether the Plymouth portion was genuinely a component of the 'ACE' or not, that portion was discontinued in 1963, and the last 'ACE' of all ran on 5 September 1964.

North Road station, 23 August 1961. The rebuilding of the station is virtually complete, although the ceremonial reopening didn't take place until March the following year. An up train, hauled by D602 BULLDOG and including what appears to be a GWR restaurant car, pulls away from Platform 7. PHOTOGRAPH: R.C. RILEY

Saltash station, 10 August 1962. It has been well documented elsewhere that DMUs took over on the 'Saltash Motor' services in June 1960 and the reason behind this steam working is something of a mystery - presumably a late diesel failure. Whatever the story, lined green 0-6-0PT No.6430 waits at Saltash with the auto-train for Plymouth - when these services were exclusively steam-worked, it was usual for the engine to face smokebox-first on the down trip (i.e. pulling), returning bunker-first (pushing). The train formation seen here was standard, but at peak times during the steam era, the 'Saltash Motors' had often been boosted to four carriages - two in front of the engine and two behind. The opening of the Tamar Road Bridge in 1962 brought about a vast improvement in local road communications, and the Saltash local services - or what remained of them - ceased in April 1972. PHOTOGRAPH: W. POTTER

Royal Albert Bridge, 25 July 1962. The Tamar Bridge, which carries the A38 trunk road across the river, was officially opened by HM The Queen Mother in April 1962. Whatever one thought of its appearance, it provided a desperately-needed route to Cornwall. Previously, the local crossing was by means of the Saltash Ferry while through traffic used the Torpoint Ferry - once experienced at peak season, never forgotten! Although the Saltash Ferry met its inevitable demise after the road bridge opened, the Torpoint chain ferry (much nearer the southern reaches of the Hamoaze) continued operating and, in fact, prospered. There had, incidentally, been a chain-guided ferry at Torpoint since 1834. It has often been remarked that the new bridge clashes horribly with the historic Brunel structure alongside, but to be fair to the planners they weren't exactly spoiled for choice when it came to a location for the road bridge.

Saltash, 23 September 1960. As from Monday 13 June 1960, the Plymouth - Saltash suburban autos were replaced by diesel units. Here, a Birmingham RCW three-car set waits at Saltash while No.4087 CARDIGAN CASTLE restarts from the up home signal (just west of the station) with a Plymouth-bound train. PHOTOGRAPH: R.C. RILEY

Royal Albert Bridge, summer 1970. For our final look at the Plymouth area we enter the 1970s - but only just. Yellow-fronted 'Warship' No.816 ECLIPSE (now without the 'D' prefix) comes off the Royal Albert Bridge into Saltash station with the 5.10pm Plymouth - Penzance. This was always a very popular viewpoint for pictures of one of Britain's most famous railway landmarks - the Royal Albert Bridge - but since the early 1960s the view hasn't been quite the same...

Railtours

Plymstock, 2 May 1959. The RCTS 'Brunel Centenarian' railtours incorporated an 'O2'-hauled trip along the Turnchapel branch with No.30182 and a two-coach auto set formed by gated trailers S738S and S2622S - this is the Turnchapel platform at Plymstock. The locomotive wears the 72C shed-plate of Yeovil Town, having been recently transferred there from Exmouth Junction. PHOTOGRAPH: HUGH BALLANTYNE

North Road station, 3 May 1964. The RCTS/PRC special, 'The Cornubian' - the last steam-hauled train to Penzance - was worked from North Road by unrebuilt Bulleid Pacific No.34002 SALISBURY. The locomotive's cosmetic perfection was courtesy of members of the Plymouth Railway Circle, who had toiled overnight at Laira. PHOTOGRAPH: HUGH BALLANTYNE